VIRGINIA HAMILTON

America's Storyteller

VIRGINIA HAMILTON

Julie K. Rubini

BIOGRAPHIES FOR YOUNG READERS

Ohio University Press

Athens

Ohio University Press, Athens, Ohio 45701
ohioswallow.com
© 2017 by Ohio University Press
All rights reserved

Printed in the United States of America
Ohio University Press books are printed on acid-free paper ⊗™

27 26 25 24 23 22 21 20 19 18 17   5 4 3 2 1

Frontispiece: Virginia Hamilton and one of the frogs from her collection.
© *2016 The Arnold Adoff Revocable Living Trust*

Library of Congress Cataloging-in-Publication Data

Names: Rubini, Julie, author.
Title: Virginia Hamilton : America's storyteller / Julie K. Rubini.
Description: Athens, Ohio : Ohio University Press, 2017. | Series:
  Biographies for young readers | Includes bibliographical references.
Identifiers: LCCN 2017006568| ISBN 9780821422687 (hardback) | ISBN
  9780821422694 (pb) | ISBN 9780821446010 (pdf)
Subjects: LCSH: Hamilton, Virginia, 1936–2002—Juvenile literature. |
  Authors, American—20th century—Biography—Juvenile literature. | African
  American authors—Biography—Juvenile literature. | Children's
  stories—Authorship—Juvenile literature. | BISAC: JUVENILE NONFICTION /
  Biography & Autobiography / General. | JUVENILE NONFICTION / Biography &
  Autobiography / Women.
Classification: LCC PS3558.A444 Z85 2017 | DDC 813/.54 [B] —dc23
LC record available at https://lccn.loc.gov/2017006568

Contents

Author's Note

I'VE KNOWN of Virginia Hamilton for a long time. I knew she was an amazing author. I was also aware that she had received every major award in children's literature.

A number of years ago, I attended the Virginia Hamilton Conference, which was established while she was still with us. The event continues as the longest-running conference to focus exclusively on multicultural literature for children of all ages.

I went to the conference specifically to meet author Angela Johnson. Angela was a participating author that year at the conference. (Years later, Angela received the Virginia Hamilton Literary Award.) My husband and I had established a children's book festival in memory of our late daughter, Claire. We wanted Angela to join us at Claire's Day. I attended the event and convinced Angela to share her talent at our festival. (It didn't take much effort.)

While attending the conference, I was amazed at how much I *didn't* know about Virginia. So began my journey to learn more about this incredible writer, mother, presenter, wife, and human being.

Along the way, I've come to know the characters that Virginia created. Mayo Cornelius Higgins. Zeely and Geeder. Junior Brown and Buddy Clark. Thomas Small. And so many more.

I've come to know her husband, Arnold Adoff.

And I've come to know a woman who wore many labels on her chest, and wore them well. I wished I had been given the chance to meet her. Yet, after a great amount of time researching and writing about her life, I feel as though I have.

I hope you feel the same after reading *Virginia Hamilton: America's Storyteller*—Virginia's story.

And that you feel inspired to read her magnificent work.

VIRGINIA HAMILTON

CHAPTER ONE

CHARACTERS

. . . it was just my good luck to have descended from a slew of talkers and storytellers—plain out-and-out liars at times— who did not merely tell stories, but created them when they forgot parts of real stories or family history, who in effect, recreated who they were and where they came from and what they would become through acts of imagination.

V IRGINIA HAMILTON was born into a family of storytelling characters.

Their stories swirled around her like the summertime fireflies that flitted on her family's land in Yellow Springs, Ohio. Their stories illuminated her mind with images of slavery, family, adventures, home, and freedom. Their stories floated into her imagination, their glow staying with her for years after.

When their memories of real events faded, Virginia's family would get creative with their tales. She referred to this gray area between fact and, well, not quite so much, as Rememory. Virginia defined it as "an exquisitely textured recollection, real or imagined, which is otherwise indescribable."[1]

As every story needs someone to tell it, let's begin Virginia's with those who would create these rememories.

The **patriarch** of the family was Levi Perry, Virginia's grandfather.

Levi was just five years old when his mother, Mary Cloud, smuggled him into Ohio. Mary and Levi were living as slaves in Virginia. In 1857 Mary escaped and traveled from Virginia to Jamestown, Ohio, by the **Underground Railroad**.[2]

Many Perry family members had settled around Jamestown in the flat farmlands of the southwestern part of the state. Once safely there, Mary left Levi with relatives and was never seen again.

Levi was taken in and thrived among his family members. As a young man, he met and married Rhetta Adams. Her family members were also freed slaves and had settled in nearby Yellow Springs. The family took root and grew. Levi and Rhetta's family blossomed as well: they had ten children. And at least once a year, all his children heard the story of how Levi came to live in Ohio.[3]

Levi would gather Virginia's mother, Etta Belle, and her siblings and tell how his mother brought him home to his family. "Set down, and I will tell you about slavery and why I ran, so that it will never happen to you."[4]

"And this was the original story as far as I'm concerned," Virginia said. "That was the beginning of the family culture and, after that, storytelling must have been in that family from early on, because everyone told stories."[5]

As Levi was just a child when they escaped, details of the journey were as fleeting as the fireflies. The power of the story was in the accomplishment. Mary's actions provided freedom for Levi and his children.

Virginia remembered taking walks with her Grandpa Levi, holding on to his fist. His hand was permanently closed into a fist and scarred from a fire in the gunpowder mill where he worked as a younger man. He would lift her up and swing her around, and around, Virginia giggling away.[6]

"I knew him as this old friend, chewing tobacco, barely five feet tall, who, at eighty, could jump from a standing-still position into the air to click his heels together three times and land still standing. Never ever could I do that."[7]

ETTA BELLE PERRY HAMILTON, VIRGINIA'S MOTHER
© 2016 The Arnold Adoff Revocable Living Trust

Years later when Virginia won the Coretta Scott King Award for her book *The People Could Fly: American Black Folktales*, she honored her grandfather in her acceptance speech. She told the audience, "Levi Perry's life, or the gossip about his days, has elements of mystery, myth, and folklore. . . . It is from hearing such tales that I became a student of folklore."[8]

As loving as Levi was, he was also strict as a father.

Virginia's mother, Etta Belle, rebelled against Levi's rules. Levi insisted when she began dating that she only go out with ministers. Etta Belle was so upset with his restrictions that she once jumped out a window and ran away. Eventually, Etta Belle moved away from Yellow Springs, to Detroit. While there, she traveled to visit her sister Bessie and Bessie's husband in Canada. The trip would change the course of Etta's life.

KENNETH HAMILTON, VIRGINIA'S FATHER (*FIFTH FROM LEFT*)

Bessie's husband had a friend, a handsome man named Kenneth James Hamilton.

Kenneth had graduated from Iowa State Business College in the late 1890s. Back then, not many young black men completed high school, much less college. After obtaining his degree, Kenneth was told by his mother, a cook for a prominent banker, that there was a position for him at the bank. Kenneth dressed up in a suit and tie to apply for the position. He walked into the bank, prepared for perhaps his first job as a teller. Instead of being shown to the customer counter, however, he was given a mop and bucket. Kenneth walked out of the bank.[9]

Kenneth began traveling the country, playing his **mandolin**, and working various jobs, from serving on the wait staff at the Palmer House in Chicago to holding a position as a porter on the Canadian Pacific Railway.

One night during her visit with Bessie, Etta went to a dance hall. Ballroom dancing was quite popular then. Kenneth was an excellent ballroom dancer. He waltzed into the room to an orchestral rendition of "Bye, Bye, Blackbird" and Etta decided right then and there that he was the man for her.[10]

They fell in love and married. Kenneth wanted to move to a big city, but Etta felt drawn to return to her home and family. They came back to her land in Yellow Springs. Kenneth drew on his work experiences and settled into a job as the headwaiter of the Tearoom, the dining hall at Antioch College. Kenneth eventually became manager of the hall, and was beloved by teachers as well as students.

Etta and Kenneth started their own family, raising their five children on the twelve-acre farm.

Their youngest was a little girl with dark wavy hair, big hazel eyes, and the beautiful light-brown skin of her ancestors. Born on March 12, 1934, she was named after her grandfather Levi's home state, Virginia. She listened to her parents weave tales during the day and fell asleep at night to the sounds of her mother's lullaby. "Rockabye baby-bye, sleep little tot . . . I'll rest you in the elm shade when the day gets too hot."[11]

Virginia benefited both from being the youngest child and from having older parents. Etta Belle was in her forties and Kenneth in his fifties when Virginia was born. She was "spoiled" when she was young and allowed a lot of freedom to play with her cousins. Yet her parents had high expectations of her.

"My mother, Etta Belle Hamilton, was a perfectly round, small woman, not five feet tall. . . . She had a commanding presence, and a stern look from her could stop me cold. She was awfully good to me though and a wonderful teller of tales. I did my best to please her," Virginia wrote.[12]

Beautiful and determined Etta Belle could "take a slice of fiction floating around and polish it into a saga." She'd say things to her little ones like, "God doesn't love ugly" and "Don't care won't have a home."[13]

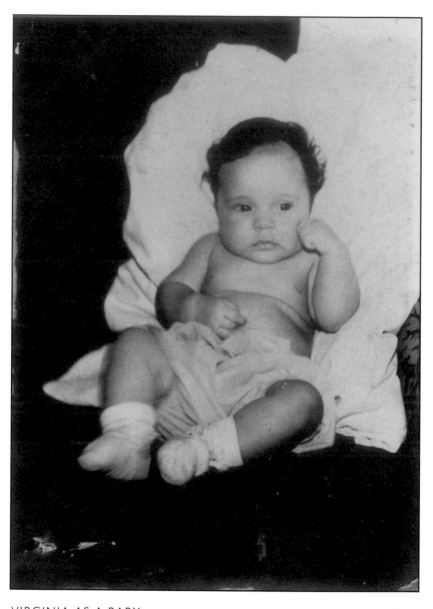

VIRGINIA AS A BABY

Virginia's older sisters and brothers were off to school at the break of dawn. Little Virginia tagged along with her mother while she took care of household chores, including tending to six hundred leghorn chickens.

As chicken was a staple in their evening dinners, Etta knew how to "ring a chicken"—taking hold of the bird's neck and twirling it around and round until the body separated from the head. The sight disturbed Virginia's brothers and sisters.

Virginia didn't mind.

"It sounds cruel, I know. But chickens were the food we ate, like vegetables. What we didn't grow or raise, we didn't eat."[14]

Etta also grew tomatoes and cucumbers and sold them, along with the eggs, to the local grocery. The money she earned from the sales she called "Extra."

"And Extra money meant new Easter coats or new school clothes for the children," Virginia said.[15]

Her mother would fill her little ears with tales that made their way into her heart—folklore such as "Br'er Rabbit and the Tar Baby." Whenever she finished a tale, Etta would say, "Be it bowed, bended, my story's ended."[16]

Virginia's father was the one with "the Knowledge," stories of African American heroes. Virginia's father opened up the world to her, by teaching her about others who came before her and accomplished great things.

Kenneth would take off his white work jacket from his job at the Tearoom, loosen up his tie, and share his wisdom. Virginia sat on her father's lap and listened to his soft, modest voice teach her about baseball player Jack Johnson, who played for and managed the Kansas City Giants in 1910 and 1911. And, as Virginia liked to sing, he'd thrill her with stories about Florence Mills, a cabaret singer, dancer, and comedienne, and Blind Lemon Jefferson, a blues and gospel singer.[17]

Kenneth told her stories about Paul Robeson and William Edward Burkhardt Du Bois, otherwise known as W. E. B. Du Bois, two men she would write biographies about later in her life.[18] Paul Robeson was a handsome and talented athlete, actor, and lawyer who was an international activist against racism. W. E. B. Du Bois was the first African American to earn a PhD from Harvard in 1895. He wrote about racism and became one of the cofounders of the National Association for the Advancement of Colored People (NAACP).

Kenneth was well read and subscribed to the *New Yorker* and *The Crisis,* the NAACP magazine. Virginia's father had many coverless, old, and musty periodicals stacked around the house. She discovered a picture of the Watusi people in one of the magazines. The Watusis are the tallest people in the world. The image stayed with her for many years, and ultimately served as the basis for her first novel for children, *Zeely.* Her father also read the Sherlock Holmes mysteries by Sir Arthur Conan Doyle. Virginia got caught up in the stories, and learned how mysteries were written and plotted as a result. These books were early inspiration for Virginia's *The House of Dies Drear,* a mystery.[19]

Of all her siblings, Virginia was closest to her older brother Bill, a dreamer. She stood by while he tried to dig a hole to China. He was certain to get to the other side of the world. She played up in the tree house he created, looking up into the Ohio sun-filled summer sky, taking in the scent of sweet, country air.

Bill had a paper route in Yellow Springs. In the winter, he pulled Virginia around on a sled as she held his papers for him. He shared his dreams for the future.[20]

Virginia played with siblings and cousins so hard that some days she was plumb tuckered out. Her cousin Marlene was her best friend and the two of them ventured through all the neighboring family farms.

"Memories of all those years, of summer days and winter nights, storms and sunshine, have given ample food to my imagination all my life," she wrote.

Words from her female relatives filled her world. "Whether while resting from the hot summer heat and enjoying sassafras tea, or warming up by the fire in the parlor on a cold winter's evening, tales were told. Tales of nature's power, about ourselves in the world, where we came from, and who we were."[21]

And, there were amusing stories told, too. There's the one about an uncle who **apprehended** the bandits who robbed a nearby bank. To the culprits, her uncle looked like a madman, with wild hair, dressed in his pajamas and shooting two pocket pistols at them. To avoid him, they dove into an empty well, breaking their arms and legs. The uncle was beside himself and fell into the well after them.

Then there was the one about how, back in 1938, Virginia's Aunt Leah was listening to the radio on Sunday, October 30. Orson Welles was on the air. His broadcast of an adaptation of H. G. Wells's *War of the Worlds* was in progress. Wells's story tells of an invasion of Earth by Martians. The radio play suggested that the invasion was actually taking place. The show created panic all over the country, including in many of the Hamilton and Perry households. Aunt Leah, being very superstitious, roused family members "in three counties." She, along with many male relatives, policed the skies throughout the night, shooting at anything that moved. Virginia's family was much more reserved in their approach. They sought shelter for hours in Grandpa Perry's root cellar.[22]

There were stories, always stories, being told by and about the many characters in Virginia's extended family.

But, just as a firefly's light dims, so too can stories that are passed on through word of mouth.

Virginia didn't remember telling stories as a child. She did not spin a yarn as her relatives did.

Virginia's gift was capturing the essence of her family's storytelling magic in her writing. She began putting her stories down on paper from an early age.

When she was nine she began "The Notebook." This journal included secrets that her parents and other family members whispered about. Little Virginia was not expected to understand the gossip shared among the elders. She took notes, hoping to comprehend the mysteries when she grew older. Sadly, she lost her journal a year later. The family secrets remained as such in Virginia's mind.

THE UNDERGROUND RAILROAD
AND ELIZA HARRIS

THE UNDERGROUND RAILROAD was a secret network of homes, churches, and farms throughout the North and South that provided safety and shelter to the thousands of runaway slaves seeking freedom. Slavery was legal in the United States from 1619 until 1865 when the Thirteenth Amendment to the Constitution abolished it. In the early 1800s **abolitionists**—people who wanted to eliminate slavery —began a network of "stations," safe locations for runaway slaves. Ohio, Virginia's home state, had more than two hundred safe houses.[26]

Just as Virginia's great-grandmother escaped slavery with her young son, so too did a woman named Eliza Harris. Eliza lived in Kentucky, just south of the Ohio River. Eliza was left with just one child after her other two children died very young. When she learned that her slave owner was going to sell her and her baby to two different owners, Eliza decided to try to escape. Eliza took her baby in the middle of a winter's night and walked to the Ohio River. Some winters the river froze solid. However, as Eliza discovered in the early morning hours, the Ohio was only partially frozen. Ice chunks floated by. With slave hunters hot on her trail, Eliza jumped from one ice floe to another to get to the other side. Sometimes she had to toss her baby on to the next floating ice chunk and then jump into the freezing cold waters and pull herself up onto the ice with her child. Eliza escaped the slave hunters and eventually made her way through the Underground Railroad to freedom in Canada.[27]

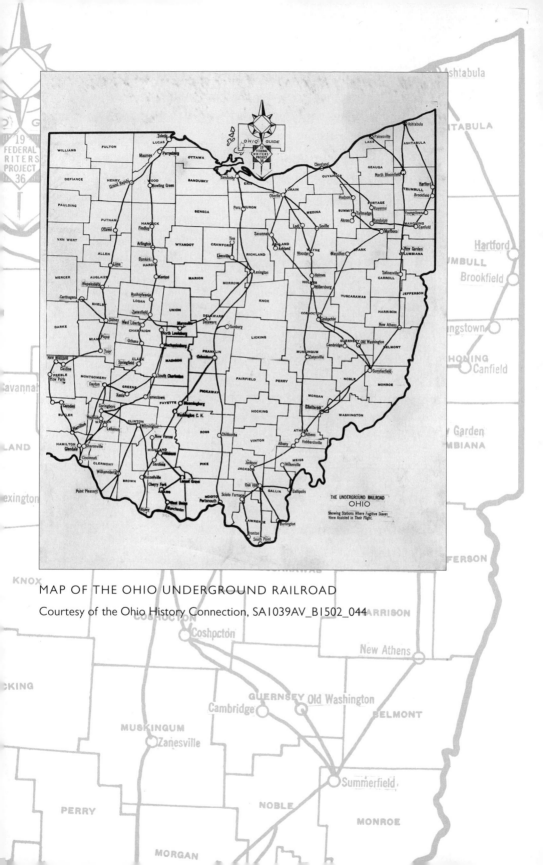

MAP OF THE OHIO UNDERGROUND RAILROAD

Courtesy of the Ohio History Connection, SA1039AV_B1502_044

Virginia set aside her sadness over the loss of her journal and turned to writing her first novel. She stretched out on the slanted, hot tin roof of the hog barn and wrote. She filled page after page with passionate prose under the scorching summer sun.[23]

As she grew older, Virginia was determined to write for a living. "I never thought seriously of any other career."[24]

That same little girl from Yellow Springs, the one who sat at her grandfather's knee and heard the story of his escape, who listened to her mother's tales and learned about her father's heroes, did become a writer. Just like the firefly that shares its light with the world, Virginia released her stories.

Boy, did she ever.

Virginia became *the* most honored author of children's literature.

Her forty-one award-winning books drew upon her family's accounts of events, both true, and some not so true.

She graced us with stories of characters who lived in her native Ohio, and those who lived in her ancestors' land of Africa. Virginia wrote of the horrors of slavery and the joys of family. She created worlds of fantasy and reflected both urban and rural landscapes in her books. Her stories were as diverse and as special as she was.

"I write books because I love chasing after a good story and seeing fantastic characters rising out of the mist of my imaginings. I can't explain how it is I keep having new ideas. But one book inevitably follows another. It is my way of exploring the known, the remembered, and the imagined, the literary triad of which all stories are made."[25]

But it wasn't easy becoming the award-winning author so many have come to love. How did she go from the carefree little girl listening to her family's stories to the amazing writer she was? What obstacles did she face along the way?

As grandfather Levi Perry would say, just sit down and let me tell you a story.

Virginia's story.

SLAVE PEN IN THE NATIONAL UNDERGROUND RAILROAD
FREEDOM CENTER

From the Collection of the National Underground Railroad Freedom Center

DID YOU KNOW?

The National Underground Railroad Freedom Center
opened in Cincinnati in 2004. Visitors can learn the stories
about freedom's heroes, from the time of the Underground
Railroad to the modern day. A "slave pen," a 21-foot by 30-
foot, two-story building that had originally served as a holding pen for slaves until they were sold at auction, is found on
the second floor of the museum.

CHAPTER TWO

SETTING

My subject matter is derived from the intimate and shared place of the hometown and the hometown's people.

I f VIRGINIA's family provided the foundation for storytelling she became known for, Yellow Springs provided the backdrop for her tales.

Yellow Springs was the place where little Virginia ran home on the last day of the school year, very excited. In her small hands was a prized possession, a book. It was bright and shiny, with three cute yellow ducks on the cover. She'd won it as a result of having read the most books in her class.

It was Virginia's first award, and treasured. New books were hard to come by in her family.[1]

Virginia loved to read.

Yellow Springs was the place with the quaint library that nurtured Virginia's passion. "It was a lovely little cottage," Virginia recalled, "shaped like a gingerbread house and made of gray fieldstone, with a red tile roof."[2]

YELLOW SPRINGS LIBRARY DURING VIRGINIA'S CHILDHOOD

Photo courtesy of Antiochiana, Antioch College

Her love for the Yellow Springs Library began with a quest to find out more about an exotic breed of chicken her mother had sent away for.

Virginia's mother encouraged her to "look at the rainbow layers" of the eggs from their **Araucanas** chickens. While the chickens roamed about in the yard, Virginia explored the henhouse.

She discovered the nests held eggs of a variety of colors. Her mother's exotic chickens laid eggs that were turquoise, pink, olive green, and various shades of brown.

"When I told my class at school about my job as colored-egg gatherer, some of the town kids snickered, 'Both you and the eggs are colored!'"

"I told Mama and she said, 'Go take a look in the library.'"

"'For what?'" I wanted to know," Virginia said.

"'For the rainbow layers,' Mama said. 'There's more than one kind of chick with color. More than Araucanas.' And then she gave me what I thought of as a secret smile."[3]

And so it was that Virginia became a regular visitor to the local library.

She even thought the "spritely, bright-eyed" Story Lady lived at the library. Once a week the Story Lady visited Virginia and her classmates in elementary school. She walked them across the street and introduced the children to her world of books.

"I'd get side-swiped every time by all those straight-back sentinels in long still rows," said Virginia. "Short books and tall books, blue books and green books. What's in them? I would wonder. They had more colors than the rainbow-egg layers ever thought of. And a greater supply of subjects. Today I realize that was my mother's point. Get Virginia to the library and she will find out many things."[4]

Yellow Springs was the place where Virginia roamed freely and played in the surrounding fields and farms owned by her family. She ventured beyond her family's lands and on to the other side of town and the glen, now known as Glen Helen, a thousand-acre preserve.

"In the glen I discovered deer, the sweet and yellow freshwater springs, an immense, condemned pavilion once a grand hotel and marvelous old vines strong enough to swing on."[5]

The images stuck in Virginia's mind and came out in two of her works. *The House of Dies Drear* features an old, spooky house, and the swinging vines appear in *M.C. Higgins, the Great.*

Through the same lands that Virginia ran as a child, Native American children had run years before. The Native Americans laughed and played as she did, chasing shadows in the woods, and picking wildflowers to take home to their mothers.

These same lands were where white settlers hunted and welcomed Ohio into the Union in 1803.

Ohio outlawed slavery in its 1803 Constitution.

However, the legislature passed "Black Laws" that discouraged migration to the state.[6] The laws were intended to make life so miserable for African Americans that they would not use the new free state as a refuge from slavery. Blacks coming into Ohio were required to show a certificate of freedom. Those who already lived in the state had to register with a county clerk. African Americans living in Ohio could not work in the state unless they possessed the freedom certificate. There was also a state fugitive law that allowed slave owners from other states to come into Ohio and capture their former slaves without interference.[7]

But, despite the restrictions, many slaves found freedom traveling via the Ohio River and settling in the area.[8] Yellow Springs was the place where many African American families bought property and built their homes.

Early residents of color may have been encouraged by the fact that Horace Mann, Antioch College's first president, was in favor of eliminating slavery.

So it came to be that Virginia's relatives, the Perrys and the Hamiltons, established their farms here.

Yellow Springs was the place where Virginia first experienced racism.

Virginia grew up surrounded by her extended family, comfortable in their presence, unaware of the division that existed.

Along with playing all day in summer, Virginia and her cousin Marlene became young entrepreneurs. They picked berries in the morning and sold them along the roadside, earning money to catch a movie at the Little Theatre.

The Little Theatre, now known as the Little Art Theatre, sits on Xenia Avenue, just a hop, skip, and a jump from the library. Marlene and Virginia rode their bikes the five-minute trip up to the theater, the smell of popcorn luring them in. Imagine their excitement at seeing movies on the theater's big screen. When Virginia first started going to the theater as a younger child, she and Marlene were not free to choose just any seat. They had to sit in the back two rows of the theater.

Only whites were allowed in the front.

In 1942, when Virginia was eight years old, that changed.

THE LITTLE THEATRE IN YELLOW SPRINGS
Photo courtesy of Antiochiana, Antioch College

The new owners of the town newspaper, the *Yellow Springs News*, Ernest and Elizabeth Morgan, ran an editorial about the separation of blacks and whites in the town. "We all know that much discrimination is practiced in Yellow Springs. The theatre, restaurants, even the Churches, find themselves doing it."[9]

The editorial hoped that this could change through "steady education" and in a "friendly way."

Students from Antioch College and faculty from Wilberforce, the first private African American college in the United States, staged a creative and peaceful approach to eliminate the segregated seating in the Little Theatre.

The students arrived thirty minutes early for a movie. The black students sat in the section designated for blacks. The white students sat

CHILDREN AND THE
CIVIL RIGHTS MOVEMENT

CHILDREN AND young people played an important role in the civil rights movement. In early May of 1963, hundreds of students of all ages marched in Birmingham, Alabama. They wanted to end the segregation that existed in their city. Children and their families could only go to fairgrounds on "colored days." They weren't allowed to visit city parks, which they supported with their taxes. Blacks had to use separate restrooms, fitting rooms, and even drinking fountains. Young people marched and rallied against this separation and inequality. Police responded by taking protesters, some as young as nine years old, to jail. Firemen used high-pressure water hoses to try to disperse the crowds. And, in a very famous image, police dogs attacked a seventeen-year-old who defied the anti-parade ordinance the city had enacted. The image landed on the front page of the *New York Times*. This photograph and reports of the violence concerned the president of the United States, John F. Kennedy. Ultimately, through negotiations, the city agreed to desegregate lunch counters, restrooms, fitting rooms, and drinking fountains. Children helped make a difference.[10]

as they normally would. Then slowly, black students moved to the white section. Whites went to the back and sat.

The owner was overwhelmed with the shifting of students, and couldn't do anything about all of the patrons moving about.

The owner complained to the mayor, the police department, and, even, a county judge. But the city officials would not do anything about the situation because no laws were broken.

The owner took down the rope that separated the blacks in the back from the whites in the front.

VIRGINIA (*SECOND FROM THE BACK*) AS A YOUNG WOMAN OUT
WITH HER COUSINS

From that point on, Virginia and Marlene could watch movies in
the theater wherever they wanted.

The town of Yellow Springs is where Virginia was formally educated. Virginia was one of only a few black students through her early
school years. Her older siblings, including sisters Barbara and Nina,
and brothers Buster and Billie, preceded her in the Yellow Springs
school system. So too did her cousins. But otherwise, there were few
African American children at the schools.

When she began attending Bryan High School, hers was the only
non-white face smiling from pictures of the cheerleading squad.

Virginia did not seem to be troubled by this. She just always tried
to do her best.

"If our white classmates were proper, then we were more so," Virginia later wrote. "If they were bright, we felt we had to be smarter, and
often we were smarter and we were proud of ourselves for showing that

"Prince Of Peace" Speakers Vie For Title

COUNTY WINNERS of the "Prince of Peace" declamation contest vied for the regional title yesterday at Belmont EUB church in Dayton. Winner was David Stull, of Cincinnati, who spoke on "The Road to Right." Alternate was Florence Thress, of Middletown. Seated, left to right ~~~ Virginia Hamilton, Yellow Springs; Marilyn Maxwell, Greenville, and Patricia C~~ and ~~ ettysburg. Second row, left to right, are Dean Miller, West Alexandria; Bar~~~isener, Springboro; Miss Thress and Stull. Semifinals will be held in Columb~~ ~~d of January.

VIRGINIA RECEIVES RECOGNITION FOR A SPEECH CONTEST

we were as good as they were. But, oh, how terrible for children to always have to think this way. What an awful toll it took on our spontaneity."[11]

Virginia was a good student, obeying one of the few rules her mother had, to stay on the honor roll. She played basketball, had a number of friends, and often got together with her cousins for fun.

She was writing and participating in speech contests, too. And she was being recognized for her efforts.

THE OHIO CIVIL RIGHTS ACT
OF 1959

THE SIGN stating "We cater to White Trade Only" hung in the window of a restaurant in Lancaster, Ohio, in 1939. The peaceful protest at the Little Theatre by the students and faculty from Wilberforce and Antioch Colleges happened in 1942. Yet, a law that prohibited discriminating against people of other races in public facilities was passed years before, in 1884. The law was not very effective in private businesses. The Ohio General Assembly enacted the Ohio Civil Rights Act of 1959. Along with eliminating discrimination in employment, the act also guaranteed all persons access to public facilities and private businesses.

SIGN ON A RESTAURANT IN LANCASTER, OHIO

Photographer: Ben Shahn. Library of Congress, Prints & Photographs Division, FSA/OWI Collection, reproduction number LC-USF33-6392-M4

But high school accolades were one thing. Where would Virginia's passion for writing take her?

The answer was literally right up the road.

But it wasn't an easy path getting there.

DID YOU KNOW?

The United States Government did not pass the Civil Rights Act until 1964, five years after Ohio passed its legislation.

CHAPTER THREE

PLOT TWIST

*I remember one time telling my older sister that I was going to
be a famous writer someday; and of all the responses she could
have given, she said, "Oh goody, then I'll be famous too."*

VIRGINIA'S PATH to becoming that famous writer began just over
a mile away from her home.

At the end of a long day working in the Tearoom at Antioch, Virginia's father would share stories of the students he served and had discussions with. When she was in high school, Virginia began working with her father at the Tearoom. Here she met students from all around the country. Many of them were from New York City and told stories of what they loved and missed about the big city.

Both young men *and* women made their way to classes under the shadow of the twin bell towers on the campus of Antioch College. Black and white students mingled on the grounds of the college, sharing ideas and studying together. Not only was Antioch the first college to offer equal opportunities to both young men and women, it was also among the first to offer the same to African Americans.

Through her experiences while working in the Tearoom, Virginia began dreaming of going to Antioch. She hoped to study writing and, perhaps, become that famous author by moving to New York City. It was a big dream. Her parents could not afford the tuition at the private college. As the top graduating student at Bryan High School, she should have received a scholarship to Antioch.

But she didn't.

The head of the theater arts program at Antioch, Paul Treichler, and his wife, Jessie, were friends of the Hamiltons. The Treichlers did not feel it was right that Virginia did not receive a scholarship. So they **intervened**. Mrs. Treichler contacted the Jessie Smith Noyes Foundation on Virginia's behalf.

The foundation was created in 1947 by Charles Noyes in memory of his wife, Jessie. Jessie was as beautiful inside as she was on the outside. She was born in Brooklyn, New York, in 1885, the same year the world's first skyscraper was built in Chicago. Skyscrapers would play a role later in her life, as her husband, Charles, bought and sold them in New York City. One of his most famous real estate deals was selling the Empire State Building in 1951 when it was considered a "white elephant," or a building too expensive to maintain.

Jessie devoted much of her life to helping others. She was a leader with the Brooklyn YWCA, one of the first in the country. Through the YWCA, Jessie worked to eliminate religious intolerance and promoted equality for women and for all races.

Jessie died in 1936, just two years after Virginia was born.

Charles created the Jessie Smith Noyes Foundation to promote equal education opportunities for all, a policy Jessie believed in. A scholarship program was established to assist students in financial need. Mr. Noyes determined that half of the scholarships would go to black students.

Thanks to the help of Mrs. Treichler, one of those students was Virginia Hamilton.

Virginia, the scholar, was on her way. She enrolled as a writing major at Antioch College.

ANTIOCH COLLEGE TOWERS

Photo courtesy of Antiochiana, Antioch College

Virginia began to develop her unique writing style under the guidance of her professors, including Nolan Miller, who taught creative writing courses at Antioch for over fifty years. Mr. Miller wrote many short stories and had several novels published during this time. Classmate Janet Schuetz would also be of influence later in Virginia's path to being published.

Virginia and her fellow writers at Antioch often hung out with their little portable typewriters at a small coffee shop off Route 68 in Yellow Springs, crafting their stories.

After three years of study at Antioch, she transferred to the Ohio State University in Columbus as a literature major in 1956. It was there that a professor suggested she follow her dream of moving to New York City to pursue her writing career.[1] So later that year, Virginia packed her bags and left Yellow Springs, which she considered "a dead end for me. And boring. No men. Just cousins!"[2] "I left Yellow Springs to seek my fortune in the big city," Virginia said.[3]

Virginia wanted to strike out on her own, away from people who were trying to help her on her journey. Even though she appreciated their assistance, Virginia determined that the best way to move forward in discovering her own voice was to leave those she loved behind. She felt compelled to move to where she might be surrounded by writers and artists. Virginia longed for independence.

Virginia moved to the East Village of New York City, known then as the Lower East Side. She found herself living in a melting pot filled with people of Polish, Czech, and Yugoslavian descent. The streets were also filled with Eastern European Jews in their wide-brimmed hats. No one really spoke to each other. Everyone seemed to isolate themselves from one another.

In leaving her home in Yellow Springs, she left the comfort of nearby family and friends. She left the ability to roam barefoot around the fields, to hear the chirping of the crickets, and to see the dance of the fireflies.

What she initially found in New York City were noisy cabs honking their horns; the fumes from busses choking the air; and people bumping into each other on the streets, their hats casting a shadow over their eyes.

Virginia felt a bit more at home when she would go visit the Hudson River on Sunday afternoons. "My river changes uptown. It has Riverside Park along its steep banks, and the park is beautiful, full of children and dogs. All sorts of people rest, lounge, read their papers, and sing. They all needed the river the same way I did."

The river helped Virginia **transition** into her new home. Her writing improved, as she separated herself from all that was familiar to her. "My writing grew better as I grew older inside. I came to understand that the river's flow was the flow of freedom within all of us."[4]

Along with adjusting emotionally, Virginia also had to make her own way financially.

She paid the rent on her Second Street apartment by working a variety of jobs. She drew upon her many talents and her **ingenuity** to make her way. Virginia used her awareness of fabrics and her typing skills in her job as receptionist and guide at the Cooper Union Textile Museum. The Cooper Union for the Advancement of Science and Art was established in 1859. Located just blocks from Virginia's apartment, the college continues to offer an education in art, education, and architectural engineering.

The position with Cooper Union didn't pay enough money to cover her rent, so Virginia learned a new skill to help make ends meet.

Virginia went to a used bookstore on the East Side and purchased an accounting book. She taught herself accounting and got a job working for an architectural firm to pay for her living expenses.[5]

Still shy of funds to support herself in the big city, Virginia turned to a talent she had enjoyed since childhood. Singing.

The Saint Nicholas Ballroom on the Upper West Side hired Virginia to sing at night. She used her strong, deep voice as she sang with big bands, as a soloist as well as with groups.

Gradually, Virginia eased into the **bohemian** feel of the big city. And she looked the part. She went about the city wearing a black beret, a dark trench coat, and velvet slacks. "I thought of myself as a young sophisticate developing into an artist," she said.[6]

Virginia loved jazz music and befriended many musicians and singers through her own singing **gigs.** She enjoyed going to different clubs and listening to the musicians wailing on their saxophones, jamming on bass, and working their magic on the piano.

One particular club, the Five Spot Café in lower Manhattan, was a favorite. The Five Spot was just a ten-minute walk away from Virginia's apartment on Second Street.

"It was a time of cool jazz and 'shades' worn at night," Virginia said.

Virginia fit in with the hip crowd as she sat back in her seat, relaxed while listening to jazz at the Five Spot Café. She tucked a book under one arm and sipped her drink slowly. The audience didn't applaud after a song. They snapped their fingers to show their appreciation. Virginia did the same.

One such sophisticated evening at the Five Spot changed her life.

Virginia walked into the club to the sounds of Charlie Mingus, strumming on his big old bass. Wherever Charlie played, crowds gathered. Along with being an amazing bass player, Charlie was one of *the* most important jazz composers, pianists, and bandleaders. On this night at the Five Spot, cigarette smoke filled the air. Small tables, pushed close to each other, were filled with a wide variety of patrons—black, white, young, and old. All were there to listen to the cool jazz.

The tin ceiling captured the sounds and tossed them back to customers, as they tapped their toes to the music. Charlie and his band jammed on a slightly elevated stage. A bulletin board with announcements from around the Village served as the stage background.

Among the crowd was a handsome young poet and teacher. His name was Arnold Adoff, and he served as manager for Charlie. As manager, Arnold negotiated and coordinated Charlie's appearances and record deals.

Arnold and Virginia had seen each other around town. She had made quite an impression on Arnold. "She was this very distinctive young black woman," he said, "with this short cropped Afro, from a small town."

They ran into each other in New York. She often borrowed money from him, as she was barely making ends meet. He was working as a substitute teacher for New York City Public Schools, making twenty-six dollars per day. Back then it was a decent wage.

"Virginia would borrow five dollars, which would, back then, be enough for a pizza and a double feature at a theater on 42nd Street," Arnold said.[7]

Virginia and Arnold, along with other friends, spent the evening at the Five Spot Café enjoying the music together, and talking between sets. As the night drew to a close, Charlie offered to give Arnold a ride home. In turn, Arnold asked Virginia if she would like a ride to her

CHARLES MINGUS PLAYING AT THE FIVE SPOT CAFÉ, NEW YORK
CITY, 1958

© Dennis Stock/Magnum Photos

apartment. She had a friend with her, and it was late, so Virginia accepted the ride.

As Virginia and her friend exited the car, Arnold whispered, "Can I have your number?" She gave it to him. But, unlike today when you may exchange phone numbers via cell phones, the exchange was not so simple in 1958. Phone numbers back then included a series of letters based on where the person lived, as well as actual numbers. It was a bit complicated, and a little difficult to remember phone numbers without writing them down on a piece of paper.

Charlie continued to try and talk to Arnold on the way home. Arnold remained silent, trying not to forget Virginia's telephone number. He didn't.

Unable to sleep, Arnold called Virginia. They talked for hours. Arnold read poetry to her. At some point in their conversations that night, Arnold "knew that he had to spend the rest of his life with her."[8]

After talking most of the night, Arnold visited Virginia at her apartment late the next morning. She offered to cook him breakfast despite having a small refrigerator filled with not much more than "various containers filled with a little milk, and others with a little ketchup." She managed to put together an omelet made out of two eggs, a can of Vienna sausage, and a little butter.[9]

Her apartment was in what had been a tenement building in the late 1800s. Many of these buildings began as individual family homes. As their well-to-do residents began moving from the Lower East Side to neighborhoods further north in Manhattan, the buildings were divided into smaller apartments. The rooms in the buildings got little light or fresh air.

Immigrants flocked to the inexpensive apartments. Often extended families packed into the apartments so tightly that up to twelve adults slept in a room just thirteen feet across. Reforms in the early 1900s forced updates on existing buildings and restrictions on new ones.

Virginia's small space had no private bathroom. There was one down the hall, shared by residents of several other apartments. Her tiny apartment had little heat—no radiators, just a steam pipe in her bed-

HISTORY OF PHONE NUMBERS
AND DIGITS

IT IS so easy now to exchange phone numbers through cell phones. However, when telephones first came into use, telephone operators would put you in touch with whomever you wanted to call. As private phone usage greatly expanded in the 1940s, American Telegraph & Telephone (AT&T) developed direct distance dialing (DDD) to allow customers to call each other directly. These numbers included letters of the alphabet as well as numbers. Central phone offices had location names with digits that corresponded to the letter. Look at your cell phone. There are letters under numbers 2–9. In this case, the Beacon (BEA) office matching numbers would be 2-3-2. This would be followed by a four-digit number.[15]

What letters do the first three digits of your cell phone number match up to?

room. The kitchen had a bathtub in it, which she put a board over in order to use it as a table and workspace.

Virginia would visit Arnold at his apartment on Horatio Street. She would sit in his rocker and read works by William Faulkner, her favorite writer, to him. Arnold's apartment was a vast improvement over hers, with a giant fireplace, and a small mini-fridge with a stove on top of it. When it rained, however, the water cascaded down the street and into his basement apartment, through the casement window, and onto his daybed.

Virginia's apartment got broken into. Arnold invited her to move in with him. It didn't take much to convince her.

They lived and worked literally side by side from that point on.

"We bought a long door from what was called the Door Store back then," Arnold recalled. "We put on four cast-iron legs and made a table. Virginia would sit at one end writing away on her little Olivetti typewriter and I would sit at the other end, writing on mine."[10]

Despite their differences—she, a young African American woman from a small town in Ohio; and he, a white, Jewish man from the Bronx—they discovered many similarities. "We had greater differences in geography and gender than race," Arnold said.[11]

Family was important to both, yet they could only trace their roots no further than their great-grandparents. Arnold's great-grandparents never left Russia. Virginia's great-grandmother rescued her grandfather from slavery and was never heard from again. They were both separated from their past, and, therefore, conscious of creating something new and important as a result.

Both Virginia and Arnold were well educated. While Virginia was attending Antioch College and the Ohio State University, Arnold had obtained his undergraduate degree from City College in New York and his master's from Columbia University. They both loved to write, and they loved jazz music.

Most significantly, Virginia and Arnold had dreams of being successful writers. They both enrolled at the New School for Social Research. The school, founded in 1919, still offers graduate-level course work, intended to go beyond **mainstream** thought.

Arnold was studying poetry and Virginia had landed a **coveted** spot in a course with Hiram Haydn. Hiram was one of the founders of Atheneum Books, a publishing firm. His firm was established in 1959, the same year Virginia took a novel workshop with him. Arnold lent Virginia the money for the course. "I don't remember ever paying him back," she said.[12]

This **candor** was a trait that Arnold, as well as many others, admired. "She was the most honest person I ever met. She cared deeply about being honest," Arnold said.[13]

Virginia's writing took her in a direction she never envisioned during this time. A short story she wrote while in college, featuring a

RANDOM HOUSE INC.

457 MADISON AVENUE, NEW YORK 22, N.Y. TELEPHONE PLaza 1·2600

RANDOM HOUSE BOOKS · THE MODERN LIBRARY · LANDMARK BOOKS
LEGACY BOOKS · ALLABOUT BOOKS · THE AMERICAN COLLEGE·DICTIONARY

Hiram Haydn, EDITOR-IN-CHIEF

February 9, 1959

Miss Virginia E. Hamilton
128 East 2nd Street
Apt. #1
New York, N.Y.

Dear Miss Hamilton,

I am very happy to tell you that you are
admitted to membership in the Novel Workshop, Course #694, for the next semester.

The first class meets on Thursday, February
19, at 8.10 p.m. I enclose a signed form
which you will need when you register.

The material you submitted is returned here-
with.

Sincerely yours,

Hiram Haydn
Hiram Haydn

P.S. If it is possible, I would like you to
have ready for the opening class, the first
chapter of the book on which you will be
working during this semester.

hh:kc

LETTER TO VIRGINIA CONFIRMING ACCEPTANCE TO A NOVEL-
WRITING WORKSHOP WITH HIRAM HAYDN

tall, black woman resembling an African princess, impressed one of her former classmates from Antioch. Virginia based the story on an image of the Watusi tribe she saw years before in those old, musty magazines her dad had lying around the house. Virginia's story was about a woman who resembled one of those tribe members.

This former classmate, Janet Schuetz, now married to fellow classmate Les Schulman, was working at Macmillan Publishing as an ad writer.

"Whatever became of those stories you wrote in college?" she asked Virginia. "I think they'd make a great children's book."

Virginia envisioned becoming a famous writer all those years before. Yet creating children's books was not something Virginia had ever considered.

DID YOU KNOW?

Virginia loved books, even as a child. One of her favorite series was the *Nancy Drew Mystery Stories*. Virginia loved how Nancy solved mysteries, and how independent her character was.[14]

CHAPTER FOUR

VOICE

It was a happy accident—the kind of luck that hits you if you hang around New York long enough. I never really decided to write for children. It happened about the time I was thinking about giving up being a writer, since I was having trouble breaking into the adult writing field.

"I STOPPED MAKING up tales a long time ago," she said, "and now I am myself."[1]

These are the words that Zeely, a tall, regal woman, offers to eleven-year-old Elizabeth Perry. Elizabeth meets Zeely while visiting her Uncle Ross's farm while on summer break.

Zeely's words, written by Virginia, could very well apply to Virginia's discovery of her own beautiful writing voice. It was as if the combination of her new surroundings, inspiration from Arnold, and her upbringing all magically collided. Virginia's imagination, memories, and knowledge all boiled up inside her and spilled out onto her typewritten pages.

In Elizabeth, the **protagonist,** Virginia created a character much like herself as a child. Elizabeth has quite an imagination and loves to tell stories. She and her younger brother, John, are sent by train from their parents' home in the city to their uncle's farm. Elizabeth uses her creativity from the start on the train, as she informs John that he will be known as Toeboy for the remainder of the trip, and she, as Geeder.

The rural setting of the farm is much like the one Virginia grew up on as a child. Virginia brings Geeder's world alive through such vivid details as being barefoot and feeling the coolness of the dirt floor of a shed below her feet, or taking a nap amid the rows of corn, where purple morning glories climbed up the stalks.

Virginia uses the character of Zeely to teach Geeder a lesson about feeling comfortable with who she is, all the while informing her of cross-cultural heritage. Zeely, in Geeder's mind, is descended from a Watusi queen whose picture she finds in a magazine while cleaning out her uncle's shed. Geeder wishes to be just like her, until Zeely teaches her otherwise.

Just as Dorothy learns there is no place like home in the *Wizard of Oz*, so, too, does Geeder/Elizabeth learn that one should only be oneself.

Zeely was based on a short story Virginia wrote in college. The suggestion of her friend, Janet Schulman, and the guidance of Virginia's first editor, Dick Jackson, set *Zeely* toward publication and propelled Virginia into the world of children's literature.

Prior to their interest in *Zeely*, Virginia had been working on a novel for adults. Her work in progress was titled *Mayo*. The manuscript never sold to a publisher. Editors, who choose which manuscripts should move toward publication, couldn't see a black female writing about a male protagonist.[2]

Her writing career may have taken a completely different turn, had her first novel sold. Instead, Virginia focused on writing for children.

While Virginia's characters were growing and evolving, so too was her relationship with Arnold in New York City.

"It was an extraordinary time to live and work in New York City," Arnold said.[3]

Horatio Street, where Arnold and Virginia's apartment was, is on the upper edges of Greenwich Village. Strolling the "Village," in the 1950s, one would see artists, writers, students, and poets hanging out in coffee

ZEELY BY VIRGINIA HAMILTON, ILLUSTRATED BY SYMEON SHIMIN

houses. Cigarette smoke swirled around them, as they shared their latest work. By stepping inside, one could smell the aroma of coffee floating in the air, and hear the sounds of actors' voices presenting the first "Off-Off-Broadway" plays.

The cool sounds of jazz could be heard coming from nightclubs and cafés like the Village Gate and the Village Vanguard. The beat of bongo drums filled the air near Washington Park Square. Around the Square, Jackson Pollock, the famous abstract artist, began displaying his artwork. Soon other artists joined him. The Washington Square Outdoor Exhibit still takes place today, twice a year. Old men hunched over chessboards on the sidewalks, and young families pushed their children in strollers. Boys played stickball, using a stick and rubber ball, in the streets. The smells of sweet Italian ices and spicy Italian sausages spilled out from street vendors.

It *was* a great time to enjoy life as a young couple in New York City. But for Arnold and Virginia, there was work to be done, too.

The two of them continued to write on that table made of a door, surrounded by their books, placed on plywood shelves held upright by glass blocks. Virginia's collection included works by Gertrude Stein, William Faulkner, and Sherwood Anderson.

Virginia was also creating stories other than *Zeely*. She submitted them to the *New Yorker* magazine. The editorial staff was interested in Virginia's work and pursued the possibility of Virginia being a contributor. Virginia passed on the opportunity. She chose to focus on using her writer's voice in novels instead.

Virginia longed to be known as a writer, a female writer, and an American. She felt we all filled different roles, much like labels pinned on our chests. These were the labels she longed for.

After sharing an apartment for a year and a half, Virginia and Arnold decided to get married. They did not get engaged, for they didn't even have enough money for a ring. Arnold had already paved the way for this decision by telling his mother, "I've met a girl, she's black and I'm going to marry her."[4]

Virginia and Arnold were fortunate to be living in the state of New York. Unlike the majority of states, the New York state **legislature** had never passed any laws making interracial marriages illegal. Eventually many states **repealed** these laws. Yet, in 1960, it was still illegal in twenty-two states for a white person to marry a black person.

On the morning of Saturday, March 19, 1960, Virginia and Arnold stood in front of a judge in his chambers at the courthouse in Manhattan. A dozen friends and Virginia's brother Bill crowded into the room to witness their vows. Out of all those friends, no one thought to bring a camera. The memories of the day faded over time. "I always thought it was raining out that morning, and Virginia thought it was sunny," Arnold said.[5]

Even though the couple had been together for some time, Arnold was a little **unnerved**. "I was so nervous during the ceremony, that when it came time to place the ring on her left hand, I kept walking around her, trying to find her proper finger," he said.

After the brief ceremony, the wedding party went from the courthouse to Virginia and Arnold's apartment, where they celebrated with champagne.

Virginia and Arnold waited until June to take a honeymoon. Arnold was still teaching and needed to finish out the school year. They traveled to Europe in an unusual, but affordable, way. They sailed on a freighter ship.

"We took the train to Montreal and had dinner with an old Antioch and Yellow Springs friend living there. He drove us north along the St. Lawrence Seaway," Arnold said. "There was our freighter, the *Lealotte*. It had staterooms for only four passengers. The concept was very new at the time, but for something like $220 we had round-trip tickets to Europe."[6]

The young newlyweds spent nearly two weeks **traversing** the north Atlantic. The passage involved going past icebergs and rough seas to the freighter's home port of Bremen, Germany.

After exploring Bremen, they traveled to Paris overnight by train.

VIRGINIA ON THE DECK OF THE *LEALOTTE* FREIGHTER, WHILE
ON HER HONEYMOON

"We stepped off that train as the greenest Americans arriving in that city of light . . . we were thrilled . . . a dream come true. . . . Can you imagine stashing our bags on the third floor of the walkup hotel and then to Saint-Germain and the cafés? It was heaven," Arnold shared.[7]

While in Europe, Virginia continued her work on *Zeely*, with the assistance of her editor, Dick Jackson. "Dick wrote me fabulous letters that would say, 'Between this line and that line is a chapter. Think about it, Virginia.'"[8]

VIRGINIA ENJOYING A PICNIC IN THE BOIS DE BOULOGNE,
A LARGE PUBLIC PARK IN PARIS

Arnold and Virginia returned to America in late 1960 via a Yugoslavian freighter out of Casablanca. Arnold resumed teaching for a short period; then he stopped to focus on his poetry. Money was tight. The two young writers struggled. They sold everything. Furniture. Dishes. Clothes. Everything but their beloved books.

Arnold returned to teaching and writing. And Virginia resumed working on her craft. They gave each other a five-year deadline to have a book produced.

In the meanwhile, they began creations of a different kind. Virginia and Arnold became parents. Their daughter, Leigh, arrived first, their son, Jaime, next.

VIRGINIA AND HER FIRST CHILD, LEIGH, IN NEW YORK CITY

When *Zeely* was published in 1967, children and critics alike embraced Virginia's story. *Zeely* was so different from any other book written for young people featuring black characters. Most of these books focused on racial problems, such as segregation and inequality. *Zeely* was simply a delightful, enchanting story whose characters just happened to be black.

The American Library Association recognized *Zeely* as a Notable Book, the first of many honors bestowed upon Virginia's work.

The following summer Arnold taught at Connecticut College, and served as a faculty member for a special program where inner-city

A HISTORIC SUPREME COURT CASE

RICHARD PERRY LOVING and Mildred Jeter Loving were woken in the middle of the night on June 12, 1958, by a sheriff from Central Point, Virginia. The sheriff questioned the legality of their marriage, even though the Lovings produced their wedding certificate from ten days before. The Lovings were married legally in Washington, D.C. The sheriff demanded that they get up and arrested them. He charged them with disobeying Virginia's laws against **miscegenation,** or interracial marriages. The Lovings went to court to have the charges dropped. Instead, the judge found the couple guilty and sentenced each to a year in jail. He **suspended** the sentence if they moved out of the state of Virginia for the next twenty-five years. The judge indicated that they could visit the state of Virginia, but never together. The Lovings left their home and moved to Washington, D.C. Richard commuted to his job as a bricklayer, and Mildred went back to Virginia to birth two of their children. Mildred wrote a letter to Robert F. Kennedy, the attorney general of the United States, asking for his help.[9]

Her letter and their fight for justice ultimately took their case to the United States Supreme Court. The ruling on June 12, 1967, was cause for celebration. Chief Justice Earl Warren offered these words on behalf of the Court: "The Fourteenth Amendment requires that the freedom of choice to marry not be restricted by invidious racial discrimination. Under our Constitution, the freedom to marry, or not marry, a person of another race resides with the individual and cannot be infringed by the State."[10]

children were brought to the college and given the opportunity to see firsthand what a campus was like. Virginia worked on her second novel for young people, *The House of Dies Drear*. A mystery, the book draws upon Virginia's memories of her grandfather's stories of the Underground Railroad. The family lived in a quaint cottage on campus. Leigh and Jaime played with the young students attending their father's lectures.

During this time, Virginia and Arnold were ready for a change in their own setting. The Village was no longer what it used to be when they first moved there. Crime rates were up, drug use was common, and they didn't feel safe even taking their children for walks as they used to love to do. It was also now time for Leigh to start attending school, and Virginia and Arnold were not pleased with the options in the Village.

The call of home, the lure back to her roots, weighed heavily on Virginia's heart.

The Hamilton-Adoff clan decided on a move. They bought two acres of property that was originally part of Virginia's family farm just outside Yellow Springs. Virginia and Arnold built a home based on plans that Arnold found in a magazine.

This place of refuge, with all of her childhood memories, refueled Virginia's imagination.

One of the first works inspired by her return home features a young boy with the first name Mayo.

This book proved to the world that a female *could* write a story with a male as the main character.

DID YOU KNOW?

Black Is Brown Is Tan, **written by Arnold Adoff, was the first picture book published featuring a family composed of a black mother, white father, and their children. The happy story focuses on the importance of equality within a family. Although it was first published in 1973, the messages within the book are just as important today.**

BLACK IS BROWN IS TAN BY ARNOLD ADOFF

CHAPTER FIVE

FLASHBACK

Time now for the author to become a working writer and, indeed, I have. Whatever else I do—buy groceries, raise my children, take care of my husband, plant crocuses—I write each morning and each night. I think, I dream writing, and writing is who I am.

Two significant events happened in the United States in 1969. Richard Nixon became the president. Neil Armstrong walked on the moon.

That same year two major occurrences also took place in Yellow Springs. James E. Lawson was elected the first African American mayor of the community.[1] And Virginia Hamilton, Arnold Adoff, and their children, Leigh and Jaime, moved back to town.

"Having lived ten or more years in New York, I discovered that my mind had never left Ohio. And so I returned to the river and the country. I could write. I had done it. I had pulled past and present, memory and experience together and grown deep like the river," Virginia wrote.[2]

They returned to the lands where family surrounded them, to the fields Virginia loved to explore as a child, to the comfort of the small, inclusive town of Yellow Springs. Their children grew up in the same environment that inspired Virginia, safe and nurtured. Most of all, Virginia came back to the source of so many memories that ignited her creativity and productivity.

Arnold and Virginia built their modern home on two acres of property from the original Hamilton plot. Arnold's healthy tomato and basil plants flanked the front entrance. The bright foyer saw Leigh and Jamie dashing in and out over the years, and many friends and family members coming and going for visits. The family room, with its high ceiling, was lined with their treasured book and music collection. Sliding glass doors in every room on the ground floor seemed to invite what was outside, in, and what happened inside, out.

After the children went off to school, Virginia and Arnold would head to their respective offices, sometimes catching up with each other in the kitchen while refilling their cups with the coffee Arnold made that morning.

Virginia's office was on the main floor, separate from, but near enough to, the activity of their home. From here she smelled Arnold's homemade **marinara** sauce bubbling on the stove. Arnold's office was upstairs, near enough to Virginia, but separate enough that he could do his own work.

Virginia plunked herself down at her desk, looked out the glass doors to a one-hundred-year-old hedgerow, and went about the business of being Virginia. She began her day by attending to her **correspondence**. Virginia was known for her letters. Virginia's typewritten notes, at times accompanied by photographs, were filled with stories as to what she, Arnold, and the kids were up to. Virginia would often share a story behind the most recent book she was working on. Sometimes Arnold would add a little handwritten note on the border of the letter, offering his best to the recipient.

After Virginia caught up on her personal letters to friends and professional correspondence to editors, she turned to her typewriter and worked on her stories.

VIRGINIA, ARNOLD, AND JAIME IN THEIR NEW HOME IN
YELLOW SPRINGS

Virginia preferred to start working early in the morning. She felt that by doing so, she couldn't come up with excuses for not writing.

Arnold was in his office working as well. They touched base with each other, sharing their progress, using each other as a sounding board for their work.

"I measured Ginny's progress on each project by her voice floating up to me on some late afternoon or as we met in the kitchen to refill our cups. There was always time to follow her into the office, sit in my chair by the sliding doors, and listen as she read to me. I loved that process of listening to chapters of a new novel, or her new telling of an old tale."[3]

After spending most of her day writing, or working through copy-edits on one manuscript, Virginia took the time to go up to the school and pick up Leigh and Jaime. She loved to drive, for native New Yorker Arnold never did. She sometimes would end her writing day when Leigh and Jaime were home from school. Other days she'd go back to her writing.

Virginia settled into her writing and family life in Yellow Springs. As her children grew, so too did her capacity to balance writing with spending time with them. In fact, she often worked on two books at a time, as she did while writing a biography of Paul Robeson, the dashing actor, singer, and lawyer who was an activist against racism. Robeson was one of the African American heroes whom Virginia had learned about from her father, Kenneth.

Her dedication to her writing and her ultimate aspirations for her work shine through in a letter written to Ellen Rudin, her publisher with Harper Junior Books:

> Please forgive my dirty typewriter keys, but it's night and I'm out of cleaner; I do want to get this letter off to you forthwith. I received your letter of the 12th—thanks for all the nice things you said about me. I figure library and teacher folk (and most other folk) are about like me. They want to tell something personal; they want to connect.[4]

Virginia's desire to share personal stories came to the surface after she was back home in Yellow Springs. Her recollections of her childhood and living on the lands she grew up on provided clear images to Virginia's mind. And one of those visions stayed with her so long she had to write about it.

"I got a picture of a kid running through woods with lettuce leaves wrapped around his wrists," Virginia said.[5]

Virginia asked herself, "Who was this child and why was he doing this?"

"I had found my character. I just followed him to find my story."[6]

And find her character and story she did.

We first meet Mayo Cornelius Higgins, or M.C. for short, in the early morning hours on his family's land. He sits on the balcony of his home, which sits on an outcropping on what is known as Sarah's Mountain. The mountain is supposed to become *his* mountain when he grows up. But his father has said they need to leave the mountain.

Why might M.C.'s family have to leave their beloved home? Virginia creates tension within the story from the beginning, as she does with so many of her stories. There is always at least one **conflict** within her plots, yet Virginia only slowly reveals them to the reader.

M.C. sets off to the woods in the valley below to check his rabbit traps. He baits them with the lettuce he has wrapped around his wrists.

M.C. is strong and athletic. Once, he even tried to swim the nearby Ohio River. He nearly drowned in the process. His father beat him with a belt to teach him to not try that again, or, at least, to plan the attempt better the next time.

M.C. uses his strength to make his way through the woods. M.C. checks his traps. Empty again.

He **ventures** further into the woods and over a ravine on a bridge made out of vines. His friend, Ben Kilburn, as light as M.C. is brown, lives with his family in the woods. Ben swoops into the story on a vine suspended from a tree. M.C. isn't supposed to be hanging out with him. Ben is a Kilburn, after all. The Kilburn family is weird. Like

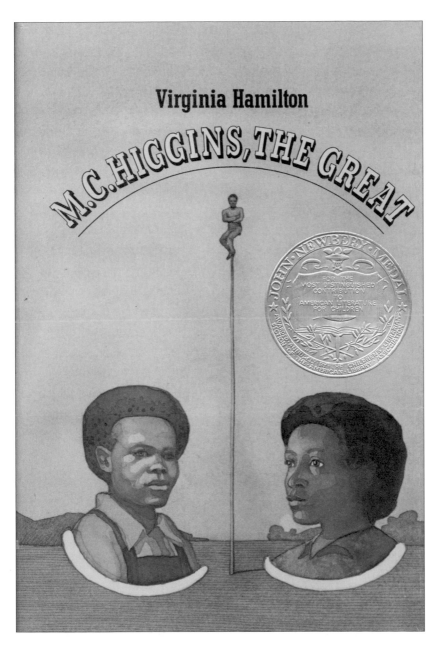

M.C. HIGGINS, THE GREAT BY VIRGINIA HAMILTON

Used by permission of Simon & Schuster, Inc.

magically weird. But Ben and M.C. have a deep connection and friendship that go beyond any concerns M.C.'s family might have.

Ben and M.C. hear bulldozers in the background. Could this be why M.C. will have to leave his mountain?

M.C. and Ben part ways, having talked about a stranger who is in the area—a man with a tape recorder. This man is recording the voices of those who live nearby. M.C. loves his momma's singing. He thinks "the dude" might want to record her voice. The stranger just might make his momma famous. Then they could leave the mountain while it is still intact.

M.C. heads for home, but not before encountering a young woman in the woods. Who is she? Is she with the strange recording man?

At home is M.C.'s special haven. A pole. With a bicycle seat on top. And two pedals and two tricycle wheels below the seat on each side. The pole sits firmly planted in a pile of junk. And from this pile of old tires, fenders, and various car parts, springs M.C.'s perch. From here M.C. can see his world changing in front of his eyes.[7]

What happens to M.C. and his family? Does "the dude" make his mother famous? What about the young girl in the woods and his friendship with Ben?

All these answers are found between the covers of *M.C. Higgins, the Great.*

Also found within the story are various elements that were all a part of Virginia's childhood experiences. Swinging vines. Rural setting. Friendships with white children. Close family relationships. Concern for the land. Storytelling.

Virginia drew upon the "known, the remembered, and the imagination" in her creation of Mayo Cornelius Higgins.[8]

Written from Virginia's new home on her old lands, *M.C. Higgins, the Great* was destined to be a huge success.

So much so that Virginia was given one of the most distinguished awards a children's book could receive—and two other significant awards.

And she made history.

STRIP-MINING IN
APPALACHIAN OHIO

SARAH'S MOUNTAIN is being destroyed in *M.C. Higgins, the Great*. Sarah's Mountain has coal lying beneath its beautiful surface. Sarah's Mountain is suffering from strip-mining.

Less than two hours away from Yellow Springs are nine thousand acres of land that had been laid barren due to strip-mining. Strip-mining is the process of clearing the land to harvest the coal that lies underneath. Problems created by strip-mining include landslides and loss of topsoil. In 1977 the Surface Mining Control and Reclamation Act became federal law. As a result, Ohio Power, the company that cleared the land to mine the coal for its power plants, was required to restore the land.

Ohio Power, with the cooperation of eight zoos from the region, reclaimed the land and created a grassy prairie with lakes.[9] Now known as The Wilds, the land serves as a preserve for a variety of wild animals.

BUFFALO GRAZE ON THE MANY ACRES OF THE WILDS IN OHIO

The Wilds/Columbus Zoo and Aquarium

DID YOU KNOW?

The Wilds, with nearly 340 mammals representing 32 different species from around the world, is one of the largest conservation centers for endangered species in North America.[10]

CHAPTER SIX

TURNING POINT

Most young people who write me tell that my books teach them things—ways to live, how to survive. Having set out to be nothing more than a teller of tales, I have come to feel more responsible—that what I have to say is more worthwhile than I had first thought.

T HE BALLROOM was filled with many of the eleven thousand attendees of the American Library Association annual conference. Those sitting and waiting for the speaker had come to San Francisco from all over the country. They were librarians, staff members, teachers, authors, and book lovers.

And they couldn't wait to hear Virginia Hamilton, the winner of the Newbery Medal for *M.C. Higgins, the Great.*

Virginia, Arnold, Leigh, and Jaime traveled by train to the conference. They avoided flying as much as possible. There was no train from Dayton, the nearest larger city. So the whole family took a Greyhound bus from Dayton to Chicago, then caught a train from Chicago to San Francisco. Little Leigh proudly pranced down the aisles of the train, a copy of *M.C. Higgins, the Great* in her hands, proclaiming, "Look, my mom wrote this book, and she's getting the Newbery Medal!"

THE NEWBERY MEDAL

Courtesy of the University of Illinois Archives

Virginia and Arnold looked **resplendent** for the event. Virginia was especially elegant in her red-and-white floor-length gown. Arnold sported a tuxedo with a black bow tie. Leigh and Jamie stayed in the hotel room with Virginia's sister and discovered the joys of room service.

Virginia had prepared for this **momentous** occasion. Her speech was ready, and so was she. She and Arnold were escorted to the head table, up on stage. Arnold was nervous. This was a big deal. He now regrets chain-smoking at the elevated table, in front of all.

Virginia took it in stride, sharing her warm, gracious, almost regal smile with the crowd. They marveled at the dinner, especially when the waiters walked in as a group, toting flaming Baked Alaska for dessert.

Virginia was a naturally shy person. She didn't like making speeches. Yet, when appearing in public, or giving a presentation, she took on a whole different **persona**. She was vibrant, outgoing—everything you wouldn't expect from a woman who much preferred to be at her desk writing, or simply spending time with her husband and children.

Much is required of a successful author, and most particularly an African American woman weaving tales written in a style never before offered to readers. Virginia met all of the requirements. Her stories

VIRGINIA AND ARNOLD, FORMALLY DRESSED, PRIOR TO THE
NEWBERY MEDAL CEREMONIES

always prevailed, whether written in her books, or delivered at the podium during a lecture or an acceptance speech.

So it was with her Newbery acceptance speech.

Virginia's comments were a true reflection of who she was as a person, a writer, a wife, and a mother.

She began by expressing her gratitude to the American Library Association and the committee who selected *M.C. Higgins, the Great* for the award. Since 1922, the medal has been given to the author of "the most distinguished contribution to American literature for children" by the Association for Library Service to Children, a division of the American Library Association.

The first award was given to a book written in 1921, then recognized at the organization's convention the following year. That tradition held true in 1975, when Virginia's book, published in 1974, was recognized as the winner.

Virginia continued her remarks, standing high above the crowd, behind a **lectern** placed on the head table covered with a shiny gold table skirt.

"In my hometown, which is a small, relatively obscure Midwestern community, my family has been, if not well known and well heeled, at least talked about from one generation to the next. My mother's large, extended, and complex Perry clan literally plummets individual Perrys into the spotlight."[1]

And then Virginia the storyteller reflected on those various characters within her family, including an uncle who drove over a cliff while trying to shoot an elk, and that other uncle who cornered the bank robbers.

The audience loved the story of the aunt who, while listening to the famous radio broadcast of H. G. Wells's *The War of the Worlds*, truly believed the world was being invaded by Martians. They laughed to the point of tears as Virginia recounted how Aunt Leah gathered up all the male relatives and spent the next six hours looking up into the sky and shooting at anything that moved.

"Don't blame me if tomorrow you discover that the three tales I've related are exaggerations. For they were told to me by other Perrys, and none of us is known to tell a story the same way twice," she said.[2]

Virginia continued sharing stories, including how touched she was by a reception the Yellow Springs branch of the Greene County Public Library held in her honor. She was particularly moved by a conversation she had with an older gentleman. He looked vaguely familiar to her, but she could not place him.

"'You may not recollect me,' he said, 'though I do recall you from a child. I am the elder Standhill, and I knew your dad, and I must say, Kenny Hamilton would have been good and proud of you upon this day.'"

She was very honored by his words, particularly since she **idolized** her father. Virginia shared her reaction with the American Library Association audience.

"Something inside me went dead quiet at the sound of the man's stark Midwestern voice, sweet to my ears and so like my own late father's stirring accent. I caught the essence of it and filed it away in that place where writers keep extraordinary human sounds, while struggling with my memory and the gentleman's not unfamiliar face."

When Virginia still did not fully recognize him, the gentleman told her to never mind. He went on to say, "What I wanted to tell you, was that we are all so proud of you. And I want you to know—we are aware of the significance of this award in the *lit'ry world*."

The elderly gentleman, his glasses fogged from the rain that had descended upon Yellow Springs days before the reception, shared how they knew each other. He had been the grocer who had allowed Virginia to treat her friends every day to bags of chips and charge them to her father's account at the store. "I'd like to think that through that small indulgence, I was the one who helped you get your way in life," he said.

These were the kind of people and experiences that had made their mark on Virginia. She continued to credit the support of her extended family in her comments to the crowd gathered at the ceremony.

Then she revealed that her work on *M.C. Higgins* was not easy. It took a long time from the initial image of Mayo Cornelius Higgins until the final sharing of his story.

"No book of mine was ever in more danger of being a failed labor of love than was *M.C. Higgins, the Great.* None was to bring me more pleasure and pain in the writing. I had worked through one chapter of *M.C.*, another, and another—when abruptly nothing more of it would come. So I put the manuscript aside, trusting my instinct, which warned me I wasn't yet ready to write this one," she stated.

M.C. Higgins was born out of a vision of a young man sitting on the top of a forty-foot pole with lettuce leaves tied to his wrists. In 1972 Virginia approached her editor, Susan Hirschman, and shared the image of this boy and her inability to move forward with his story. As they spoke, Susan asked questions about M.C. and his world, which sparked further thoughts, and ultimately the creation of the award-winning novel for young people. It was a two-year process from concept through multiple revisions to, eventually, a published book.[3]

"Susan Hirschman said, 'I love this and I can publish it as it is but if you take it back and revise, you'll have the most magnificent story,'" Arnold said.[4]

M.C. Higgins, the Great, just as with most of Virginia's works, includes symbols with layers of details. Sarah's Mountain, where M.C. lives, represents the natural world that must be saved from humankind. M.C.'s pole represents the ability to see things from a different perspective.

Yet, most significant in Virginia's books are the characters. Her beautiful descriptions, both physical and emotional, of her characters allow readers to identify with them. Although most of Virginia's characters are based on people she met as a young black woman growing up on a rural farm, children of all ethnicities relate to those characters and their stories.

Toward the conclusion of her speech, Virginia offered a story about a letter from a young female student from Toronto. "'Miss Hamilton, I

AFRICAN AMERICAN AUTHORS
AND THE NEWBERY MEDAL

FOUR AFRICAN AMERICAN authors have received the Newbery. Virginia was the first, for *M.C. Higgins, the Great*, in 1975. Mildred Taylor won the award in 1977 for *Roll of Thunder, Hear My Cry*. Christopher Paul Curtis took home the coveted prize in 2000 for *Bud, Not Buddy*. Kwame Alexander won the Newbery in 2015 for *Crossover*. Additionally, Christopher Paul Curtis has received Honor Book recognition for *Elijah of Buxton* and *The Watsons Go to Birmingham —1963*. Jacqueline Woodson has been recognized with a Newbery Honor Book Award for her memoir, *Brown Girl Dreaming*.

The three female winners, Virginia, Mildred, and Jacqueline, all have ties to Ohio. Virginia and Jacqueline were both born there, Virginia in Yellow Springs and Jacqueline in Columbus. Mildred was born in the South but her family moved to Toledo when she was little.

am white, but I just as well could be black. Either kind, I'd be okay. Your books taught me to say that."[5]

Virginia thanked those who helped her on her journey in writing *M.C. Higgins, the Great*. First and foremost came her family, including Arnold, Leigh, and Jaime.

She concluded by stating, "One final note: This event here this evening is, in part, an historic occasion. I am the first black woman and black writer to have received this award. May the American Library Association ever proceed."[6]

"It was a triumphant night for her," Arnold said. "I was so proud of her, and thrilled for the reaction from the attendees in the long reception line for her."[7]

Virginia and her family remained at the conference for several days. Virginia met many fans and signed copies of *M.C. Higgins.* It was an incredible, once-in-a-lifetime experience for Virginia.

But it was just an indication of what was to come both in Virginia's writing and in the recognition her work would receive.

DID YOU KNOW?

The Newbery Medal was the first children's book award in the world! In addition to choosing the winner, the selection committee names books considered worthy of recognition. Initially known as "runners-up," since 1971 those books have been called "Honor Books."

CHAPTER SEVEN

FLASH FORWARD

*I have this great, huge chest in which I keep all of my ideas. I
think I would say they come out of my imagination, they come
out of my memories, and they come out of all the things that
I know.*

I F VIRGINIA really did have a chest filled with ideas tucked away in
the corner of her writing room in Yellow Springs, she opened it often
to let the stories float out. Virginia's imagination, memories, and all
that she knew and experienced swirled around her and found their
way into those magical stories that she shared with the world.

Virginia's stories were so unlike any other works ever written before. Young people, teachers, and librarians—all responded to each
new book with extraordinary admiration and respect.

Virginia wrote forty-one books throughout her career. No matter
what type of story a young reader might enjoy, Virginia wrote it. Fantasy. Science fiction. Biography. Folktales. And just as Virginia received
great respect for her work, she, in turn, gave the same to her readers.

"Her work was interactive," Arnold said.

Not only were readers **entranced** by her stories, but the literary
world also took notice.

Virginia received nearly every award in her field, becoming the most honored author of children's literature.

Ever.

With the constant support and guidance of her editor, Susan Hirschman, and friend Janet Schulman at Macmillan, Virginia worked hard at developing the ideas that sprang out of that story chest.

Virginia's very first book, *Zeely*, was named a Notable Book by the American Library Association, which considered it the best of the best in children's literature for that year. It was a great achievement for any author, but even more so for someone just starting out in her career.

Inspired by a childhood memory of a "haunted" house that she passed every day and by family stories of the Underground Railroad, Virginia next wrote a mystery. *The House of Dies Drear* received the Edgar Allan Poe Award, the most prestigious in the **genre**.[1]

THE HOUSE OF DIES DREAR BY VIRGINIA HAMILTON, ILLUSTRATED
BY EROS KEITH

Used by permission of Simon & Schuster, Inc.

The House of Dies Drear introduced young readers to thirteen-year-old Thomas Small, who, along with his family, has moved from the South to an old house in Ohio. The house was formerly a station on the Underground Railroad, owned by the abolitionist Dies Drear.

Thomas learns the scary legend of how Dies Drear and the two slaves he was hiding in the house were killed by bounty hunters. Frightening events occur in the Smalls' new home, leading up to a dramatic finish to this mystery.

The idea for Virginia's fourth book, *The Planet of Junior Brown*, came while she was playing with her daughter, Leigh, in a park in New York City. Virginia saw a boy "on the hook," or skipping school. This young boy became the character Buddy in the book.[2]

Virginia dreamt up a friend for Buddy, named Junior, a three-hundred-pound musical **prodigy**. The two friends have not been to class their entire first eighth-grade semester. Yet, they've been in the school, in a cellar room where the janitor has created a model of the solar system. They eventually get caught. But what happens next?

Virginia wrote of the challenges Buddy and Junior Brown face in an essay titled "Thoughts on Children's Books, Reading, and Ethnic America." "When you find yourself up against the wall long enough, you begin to calculate your endurance against the wall. You begin to know how strong you are. You are beautiful, and you think in terms of going through the wall."[3]

Virginia could have been referring to herself, for she continued to break through walls in the literary world.

Like *Zeely*, *The Planet of Junior Brown* was named an American Library Association Notable Children's Book. But Virginia knew that this story was special. Arnold felt the same. Her editors and publisher did too. It seemed as though it was just a matter of time before Virginia won the coveted Newbery Medal, considered by many the highest award for any children's book. Arnold was so convinced that *The Planet of Junior Brown* was going to win that he bought a bottle of champagne to celebrate when they received the news.

THE PLANET OF JUNIOR BROWN BY VIRGINIA HAMILTON.
JACKET ILLUSTRATION BY JAMES MCMULLAN

Used by permission of Simon & Schuster, Inc.

But the middle-of-the-night phone call from the Newbery Medal selection committee wasn't to be. Not this time, and not for *the* medal. *The Planet of Junior Brown* was recognized by the committee, but as a Newbery Honor Book, or runner-up for the big award.

It would be four years and three books later when that champagne was uncorked, its bubbles overflowing onto the floor of Virginia and Arnold's kitchen.

M. C. Higgins, the Great received not only the Newbery Medal but also the Boston Globe–Horn Book Award for Fiction and the National Book Award. It was the first book in the history of children's literature to win all three.

These awards are the most esteemed in the field of children's literature. The Boston Globe–Horn Book Award recognizes the best in children's fiction and poetry, nonfiction, and picture books. The National Book Award celebrates the best of American literature, to expand its audience, and to enhance the cultural value of great writing in America.[4] Virginia was the first African American to receive that award for children's literature.

*

IN 1982, Virginia's book, *Sweet Whispers, Brother Rush,* was published. The story features a female protagonist, Teresa Pratt, or Tree. Tree lives pretty much alone with her mentally disabled brother, Dab. Their mother, a nurse, is only occasionally at home. Tree finds help in the form of the ghost, Brother Rush, to gain control of her life.

Virginia sometimes kept handwritten notes to help her create her characters and stories. Here are her first imaginings of the ghost character Brother Rush.

> Rush is a boy of fifteen, somewhat slow-witted.
> We first "vision" him coming down the heat-drenched road at dusk.
> He heads up the yard to Mrs. Pemberton's house to sit on the top step of her porch to rest a bit.
> Brother Rush has no place to go. Mindless, he has no thought of where he has been.

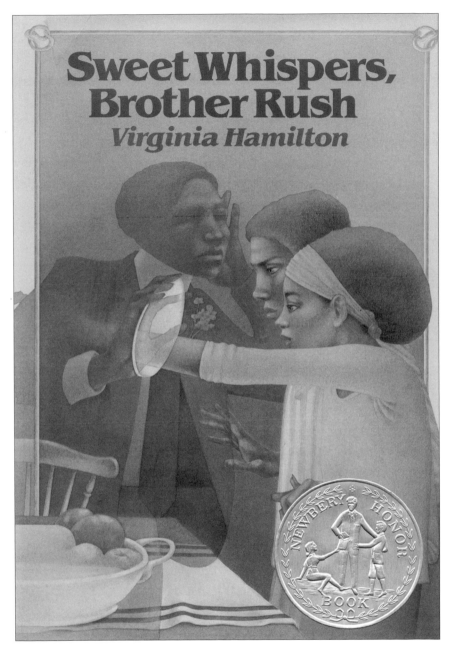

SWEET WHISPERS, BROTHER RUSH BY VIRGINIA HAMILTON.
JACKET ILLUSTRATION © 1982 BY LEO AND DIANNE DILLON

Mrs. P, old and rheumatic, reminisces behind her mucousy eyes on the past. A fleeting smile of some recognition wrinkles her caved-in face before she feels a chill and hobbles inside for her knitted porch-coat. But then a cold wind seems to climb the steps and glides over the porch to surround her.

"Death?" she whispers, and slams the door, feeling the latch, cold as ice.

Brother Rush is, of course, a ghost.

The book is about the lives he touches as he wanders the town. Brother Rush died when he was a man, but a ghost returning has no choice but to be what he finds himself.

Sweet Whispers, Brother Rush gathered recognition from thirteen different organizations, including the American Library Association and the Library of Congress. The book also received the first of three Coretta Scott King Awards that honored Virginia and her work.

The Coretta Scott King Book Awards are given every year "to outstanding African American authors and illustrators of books for children and young adults that demonstrate an appreciation of African American culture and universal human values.[5]

In her acceptance speech, Virginia concluded, "I am happy to accept this award. Its meaning for me is that I have been held accountable and found responsible. In my own way I hope to continue helping to advance among the young the cause of literacy and understanding and the cause of freedom from bigotry and prejudice, in the spirit of Dr. King and Mrs. King."

Virginia accomplished her goal of enlightening young readers in many ways. One way was by presenting new versions of old stories. Virginia's book *Her Stories: African American Folktales, Fairy Tales, and True Tales* shares nineteen different stories about African American women. Virginia sheds light on the adventures of Cat Woman, a New Orleans vampire, and Annie Christmas, a seven-foot-tall riverboat operator. Virginia shares stories created by female slaves during the plantation era. She imagines that the tales were made up by the women to entertain their children, to amuse their husbands, and to escape

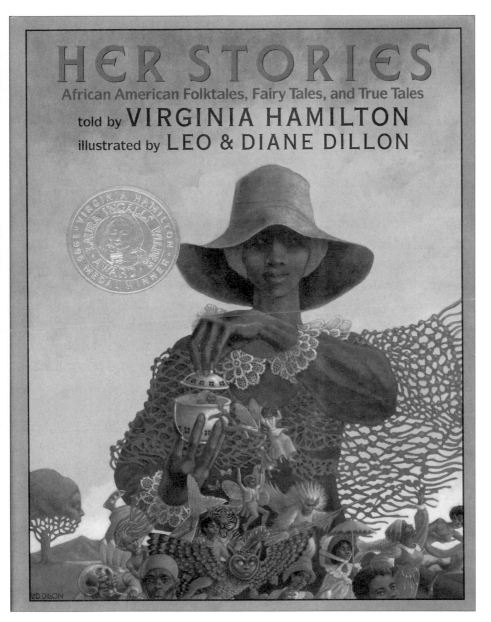

*HER STORIES: AFRICAN AMERICAN FOLKTALES, FAIRY TALES, AND
TRUE TALES* BY VIRGINIA HAMILTON. COVER ILLUSTRATION
© 1995 BY LEO AND DIANE DILLON

Scholastic, Inc./The Blue Sky Press. Used by permission

CHILDREN'S & TEEN CHOICE
BOOK AWARDS

THE CHILDREN'S & Teen Choice Book Awards is the only national book awards program in which the winning titles are selected by children and teens. This is one of the few literary awards that Virginia didn't win; the program began in 2008, six years after her death. The Children's Book Council's Every Child a Reader organization gives young people the opportunity to voice their opinions about books written for them through the Children's & Teen Choice Book Awards. In 2015, readers cast over 1.3 million votes!

from the harsh realities of their lives. The stories are meant to be enjoyed by individuals, or in group readings. "By all means, share them with one another," Virginia wrote.[6]

Virginia's stories also inspired the creation of an event in her honor that continues to accomplish her goals of creating awareness of other cultures and embracing diversity.

DID YOU KNOW?

You can vote for your favorite books! Voting for the Children's & Teen Choice Book Awards is open for about two months beginning in early March every year. Visit ccbookawards.com to vote!

CHAPTER EIGHT

FIRST PERSON

The challenge for me, the writer, is to deal with all that I consider to be the real world by creating a youth literature that beyond entertaining, shows compassion, hope, and humor. I try to provide ways to thinking, ways of opening minds to personalities.

A s Virginia's works continued to collect awards, she was in high demand to speak at conferences and even college graduations. Virginia had to constantly strive to balance her roles as children's book author, presenter, wife, and mother. Then came one invitation that she could hardly turn down.

Virginia received a letter in early December 1983. Written on Kent State University Department of English **letterhead,** it looked quite official.

The letter began:

The School of Library Science and The Elementary and Secondary Education Department at Kent State University would like to honor you for your outstanding contribution to the field of children's literature, and specifically fiction which features black characters, by creating an annual lecture to be called The Virginia Hamilton Lecture on Children's Literature.[1]

The lecture was the brainchild of members of the Kent State University English department, including Marilyn Apseloff, Anthony Manna, and Clara Jackson.

The professors had a conversation the previous winter about their shared love of children's literature. They also talked about the diversity of writers creating books for young readers. They all agreed Virginia was a "master" among such writers. They wanted not only to honor Virginia for her role in the world of children's books, but to embrace other writers and artists as well. The professors dreamed up the idea of the lecture series and, by the following winter, sent both a letter and a well-thought-out proposal to Virginia.

Virginia didn't waste any time in responding. She wrote back to Marilyn Apseloff within a week. And she did so in her gracious and amusing style.

> You certainly know how to make a girl's day! I thought one had to be dead to receive such an honor! Oh, but I am glad I'm alive and I am indeed honored and overwhelmed (is anyone ever simply whelmed?) and wondering—who me? She means me?

To emphasize how much they valued Virginia's contributions to children's literature, the committee asked her to be the first **keynote** speaker. Virginia gratefully accepted the honor, readily agreeing to speak.

> This letter sounds a bit flip. My way of cloaking slightly my deep appreciation. You guys are really something up there . . . know that I am profoundly touched by the thought and I will try to do justice to the first Virginia Hamilton Lecture in Children's Literature.[2]

The first lecture was held on April 12, 1985, at the Kent State University Student Center.

A large crowd sat in anticipation of Virginia's speech. Many in the audience had been reading her works for nearly twenty years, but had never had the chance to hear her speak. As she stood at the podium, Virginia looked every bit the regal, literary queen, sharing her stories

POSTER FOR THE FIRST ANNUAL VIRGINIA HAMILTON
LECTURESHIP

Kent State University Libraries. Special Collection and Archives

CLARA JACKSON, ANTHONY MANNA, VIRGINIA HAMILTON, ASHLEY BRYAN, AND ARNOLD ADOFF AT THE SECOND ANNUAL VIRGINIA HAMILTON CONFERENCE

Kent State University Libraries. Special Collection and Archives

with her subjects. As usual, she did not disappoint those who came to honor her. Virginia spoke about her journey as a writer in her speech titled "The Spirit Spins: A Writer's Revolution."

"It was never my design to come so far. When I started, there was no strong intent on my part, no specific direction. I had a powerful sense that I wanted to write. I thought it somewhat amusing that people would buy what I had done for free so long."[3]

Virginia spoke about her childhood. She shared how she remembered being free. She was free from work and pain. She never experienced hunger or sadness. As a little child growing up in the country outside the little town of Yellow Springs, she was free to think and to play. Her parents had just a few rules. In the summer, she was to come in from playing before dark. In the fall and winter, Virginia was to

WHAT IS MULTICULTURAL LITERATURE FOR CHILDREN?

MULTICULTURAL SIMPLY means many cultures. Literature generally means books. Put the two together, and one gets books that offer stories about different races, religious beliefs, backgrounds, and traditions for young people.

study hard, go to school, read, and listen to her teachers. She was encouraged to write everything down.[4]

And she spoke about writing for middle-grade readers.

"What I must always remember is that if there is a young person somewhere who wants to know what is in that book, who wishes to extend his or her comprehension of others unlike him or her, or simply, to find something between the covers of the book that reflects his or her personal struggles, or to find a new sort of entertainment, then the book is there for reading."[5]

The event was a success from the beginning, attracting up to five hundred teachers, principals, reading specialists, and librarians each year.

What began as a single lecture has grown into a full conference. It is now the longest-running event to focus on multicultural literature for children and young adults.

Each year several authors and/or illustrators of children's works are featured at the Virginia Hamilton Conference. During their presentations, they share the inspirations, joys, challenges, and blessings they encountered along the journey to create. Attendees wind their way through the beautiful School of Library and Information Science building to various workshops. Experts in the field of multicultural

ARNOLD AND VIRGINIA WITH CONFERENCE PARTICIPANTS IN
1999. *FRONT ROW, FROM LEFT TO RIGHT:* THE LATE WALTER DEAN
MYERS, VIRGINIA, AND ARNOLD. *STANDING, FROM LEFT TO
RIGHT:* NANCY BIRK, CURATOR OF SPECIAL COLLECTIONS FOR
THE KENT STATE UNIVERSITY LIBRARIES; CONFERENCE CO-
DIRECTORS, DR. ANTHONY MANNA AND DR. CAROLYN BRODIE;
OHIO AUTHORS AND ILLUSTRATORS, MICHAEL J. ROSEN, AMINAH
BRENDA LYNN ROBINSON, AND WILL HILLENBRAND

Kent State University Libraries. Special Collection and Archives

literature for children offer sessions on various topics such as picture
books featuring girls as the main characters, or multicultural folktales.

In 1991 the Advisory Board decided not only to invite authors, illustrators, and experts within the field of multicultural literature to
participate, but to honor them with awards as well. They established
several such awards, each given out at the conference.

The Virginia Hamilton Essay Award was the first of these awards to
be created. This award honored the author of a published journal ar-
ticle on the topic of multicultural literature.

The Virginia Hamilton Literary Award, established in 1999, is a significant recognition given to an author or illustrator who has created artistically excellent multicultural books. Walter Dean Myers, the first recipient of this prestigious honor, had written twenty-seven award-winning novels at the time of his recognition. He went on to write over sixty books for young people before his death in 2014.

The list of previous winners reads like a "who's who" of authors and illustrators of children's multicultural books. The names may sound familiar: Jerry Pinkney, Leo and Diane Dillon, Jacqueline Woodson, Ashley Bryan, and, most appropriately, Arnold Adoff.

Educators and librarians who are teaching students about different cultures and ethnicities can apply for the Virginia Hamilton and Arnold Adoff Creative Outreach Grant. Ideally, educators use books written by Virginia in their lessons.

The most recent award established is the Arnold Adoff Poetry Award. In honor of Arnold's talent and passion, the honor is given to creators of excellent poetry for elementary, middle grade, and young adult students. And, a "New Voice" award is given to an up-and-coming poet.

The annual event is still intended for educators, librarians, and adults interested in children's literature. Unfortunately, even though it is all about children's books, and features those who write them, young people can't attend. However, anyone can read the books by the amazing authors and illustrators who have participated and been honored over the years.

Angela Johnson was honored as the 2013 Virginia Hamilton Literary Award recipient. Angela has written over forty books for children and young adults, including *Toning the Sweep, Heaven,* and *The First Part Last.* She has received the Coretta Scott King Book Award for each of these books!

Angela offered her thoughts on being involved with the conference and Virginia's influence on her life as a writer.

She wrote,

Sixth Annual

VIRGINIA HAMILTON CONFERENCE

on

Multicultural Literary
Experiences for Youth

April 6, 1990
Kent State University

Keynote Speaker:
Jerry Pinkney, Illustrator

Illustration from *Mirandy and Brother Wind* by Patricia McKissack, Illustrated by Jerry Pinkney ©1988 by Jerry Pinkney.

For a complete brochure with registration form, write the
College of Continuing Studies, 204 Student Services
Center, Kent State University, Kent, OH 44242.

POSTER FOR THE SIXTH ANNUAL CONFERENCE, FROM
MIRANDY AND BROTHER WIND BY PATRICIA MCKISSAK,
ILLUSTRATED BY JERRY PINKNEY

VIRGINIA HAMILTON AND MARLENE DORSEY AT VIRGINIA
HAMILTON CONFERENCE IN 2000

Kent State University Libraries. Special Collection and Archives

When I began going to the Virginia Hamilton Conference a dream
came true. In the town that I lived in so many children's book
artists and writers came together to celebrate Virginia.

The first young adult novel I read as an adult was Virginia
Hamilton's book *Sweet Whispers, Brother Rush.* It was magical.
The book actually made me weep. I had no idea that a work of
fiction could overwhelm me as it did.

I had a very clear vision of what I wanted to do after I read
Sweet Whispers, Brother Rush. I wanted to write. I wanted to move
people's emotions like Virginia Hamilton had done for me. So
when I received the Virginia Hamilton Award a dream indeed
came true for me.

Virginia was an amazing writer. Anyone who reads her work
is reading the work of a genius.[6]

SPECIAL TREAT

VIRGINIA LOVED to eat as well as cook! At the twentieth annual conference, the committee created a cookbook of favorite recipes provided by previous participants. Here is the first entry, from Virginia and Arnold's daughter, Leigh.

"My mother Ginny, or Virginia Hamilton as some people know her ☺ named this corn recipe Ginny's Homeplace corn. My brother and I always asked for it when we came home to visit (among other family favorites but that's another story and another cookbook ☺), and it was, and still is, a staple in our family for holiday dinners. We make this baked corn dish mostly in the cold winter months, but I don't see why you couldn't make it any time of the year."[7]

Ginny's Homeplace Corn

Ingredients:

4–5 cans whole kernel corn	Ritz crackers
4–5 cans creamed corn	Butter
1 diced green pepper	1–2 T. Worcestershire sauce
2 eggs	Paprika
1 medium white onion, diced	Salt and pepper to taste
½ cup half and half	Glass 9 x 11-inch baking dish

Directions:

Preheat oven to 350–375 degrees.

Mix corn in a bowl.

Add onion, pepper, eggs, Worcestershire sauce, and half and half.

Mix together. Corn mixture should be loose but not runny.

Crumble approx. 4–5 handfuls of Ritz crackers into mixture and stir. Mixture should be moist and a bit jiggly.

Add a bit of salt and pepper to taste.

Crumble more Ritz cracker mixture for a nice crust on top.

Dot crackers with butter, and sprinkle with paprika.

Bake in oven until top is golden brown, and corn is bubbling on the top sides—about 45 minutes to an hour.

From a little girl who grew up with stories circling around her, Virginia became the most honored author of children's literature. But Virginia didn't rest. She had many more ideas that kept leaping from that ideas chest. Virginia continued to spin tales for young people. Her stories touched readers of all ages around the world.

And so that little girl who grew up on the little farm in Ohio became the woman who traveled the earth to share those stories.

DID YOU KNOW?

Arnold Adoff, Virginia's husband, received the Virginia Hamilton Literary Award in 2004. Arnold has published over thirty books for children!

CHAPTER NINE

RESOLUTION

I talk to many young people in and outside of this country,
young people from age seven or eight to sixteen and seventeen,
and I have never spoken to one of any age who did not know
somewhere inside that books and reading and writing were of
enormous importance.[*]

THE SOVIET Union. Germany. Japan. South Africa.
These are several of the stamps Virginia received in her passport
through her travels. On many of these trips, Virginia spoke to adults
about writing for young people. She also loved speaking to children of
all ages.

The first of her major trips was to Moscow in October 1979. Virginia
was one of five participants from the United States attending the Second International Conference of Writers for Children and Youth. One
hundred twenty-nine writers from thirty-nine countries took part in
the conference.[1]

The Soviet Union that Virginia saw was on the brink of war. Just
months after her visit, the Soviet Union invaded Afghanistan. Had the
invasion occurred sooner, Virginia might never have seen a country
that she first was introduced to while researching the lives of W. E. B.

Du Bois and Paul Robeson in preparation for writing their biographies. Virginia's father had taught her about both men when she was a child.

One of the most important African American activists of the first half of the twentieth century, Du Bois traveled to the Soviet Union in the late 1920s and embraced **socialism**, due to its principle of treating everyone equally.

Robeson began a career in law, but after suffering from racism in that field, turned to performing on stage, his first love. He achieved success in the United States, then moved to Europe where he became an international celebrity, a status he used to shed light on racism and injustice. Robeson traveled to the Soviet Union a number of times, and was also in awe of being treated as an equal.

Virginia learned a lot about the Soviet Union while researching the lives of the two men. She was curious about the country as a result, and longed to visit it. She was thrilled to be given the opportunity to do so when she was invited to participate in the conference.

The writers gathered from around the globe in Moscow expressed concerns about the children of the world. Poet Ismail Uyaroglu of Turkey summed up their thoughts by saying, "Unfortunately, most of the children of the earth live today in cold and hunger; they have no necessary clothes and can neither read nor write."[2]

Despite these grim thoughts, these children's authors were hopeful about the value of creating good literature for children.

The city of Moscow, with a population of eight million people at that time, seemed intent on impressing the attendees. Virginia marveled at the enormous Hotel Ukraina. The hotel's architecture reminded her of a huge crown.[3]

Virginia and her fellow attendees sat at tables with microphones and earphones offering one of seven simultaneous translations. Imagine hearing that many different languages at once.

The speakers' topics included children's book publishing in their countries, what authors were writing for young people, and trends in youth literature.

The Soviet Union was ruled by socialism. Virginia noted a "strong state control over what can and cannot be written and published."[4]

The conference included entertainment every evening. One night Virginia and her fellow writers were treated to a performance at the Central Children's Theater.

The Central Children's Theater had been created in 1918 by a young woman named Natalia Sats. When she was only fifteen years old, Natalia oversaw the founding of this theater, the first for children in Russia.[5]

Virginia was disturbed by the play, *Maximka*. It had two main characters: a Russian seaman who had lost his son in a tragedy and a young boy who had escaped a slave ship. During the play, the boy is recaptured, then resold to a rich couple who speak English. Ultimately, the enslaved boy is rescued and adopted by the Russian man who had lost his son.

The play brought many questions to Virginia's mind.

"What was I, the granddaughter of fugitives from slavery, doing in Moscow, watching a somewhat obvious lesson in class struggle and white saviors-to-the-rescue? The young woman who played the slave youth had been painted dark-skinned and wore a short, black, kinky Afro wig," she wrote.[6]

The character of the poor, sad boy **appealed** to Virginia's maternal instincts. The theme made Virginia sad. To make herself feel better, she gave the books on black contemporary literature she had brought along to her Soviet author hosts. With this small gesture, she hoped to create a greater awareness toward working to eliminating stereotypes.

After the conference officially ended, Virginia and twenty-five other authors hopped on the Red Arrow express train to Leningrad, now called St. Petersburg. Built on one hundred islands on the Neva River, the city is known as the "Venice of the North," due to all of its canals and bridges.

Virginia loved exploring the Hermitage Museum, one of the oldest and biggest museums in the world. Six buildings make up the museum complex, including the Winter Palace, the former home of Russian monarchs. The group also traveled to the town of Pushkin to visit the Catherine Palace, built in 1717 for Catherine I, empress of Russia. At the end of the day, the group enjoyed dinner (tasty beef stroganoff for Virginia) and entertainment, including a traveling circus and Western-style dinner music.

With just one full day to explore Moscow, Virginia played tourist, taking in the **Red Square** and walking within the **Kremlin.** Hundreds of people were in the square, many carrying red carnations. The flowers, which symbolized freedom, were to be placed on the Lenin Mausoleum, where the former Russian leader's preserved body can still be seen. Virginia and the crowd watched silently at the changing of the guard ceremony.[7]

After her trip, Virginia reflected on her visit and experiences. Although she didn't feel caught up in the socialistic lifestyle, the lack of chaos made quite an impression on her. She also admired the Soviet Union's dedication to children and its excellent literature for young people. "It was a privilege to have been invited to Moscow to partake of a unique mission in the interest of earth's children," she wrote.[8]

Virginia didn't take too many notes during her travels, but she did share many of her global adventures with her friend Noriko Shima. Noriko lived in Kyoto, Japan. Noriko had been a student at Claremont Graduate University in California in the early 1970s, studying Children's Literature in Education. The librarian at the George Stone Center (children's book library) told Noriko that *Zeely* was one of the most important American books then. Noriko read it and immediately fell in love with Virginia's writing.

Noriko returned to Japan after her studies, but traveled back to the United States in 1978 to see Virginia speak at a conference in Boston. Noriko had a three-year-old daughter at the time. Conference organizers told Noriko she could not come with her toddler. Virginia intervened and arranged for a friend to watch Noriko's little girl. Noriko was able to attend Virginia's presentation, and was thrilled.

Virginia took an immediate liking to Noriko, too. As a reflection of Virginia's kindness, she invited Noriko and her child to come back to Ohio and stay with her, Arnold, Leigh, and Jaime for a few days.

In a typed letter from Virginia to Noriko in August of 1978, Arnold hand-wrote a note. "Of course I echo Virginia's invitation—and add that we have plenty of room for you and your daughter to stay—and a swimming pool to help beat the usual August heat!"[9]

Noriko and Virginia kept in touch through letters for many years. In 1983, Virginia shared that she'd be traveling more in the United States that year.

"I have many trips around the country," she wrote, "New Orleans, Louisiana, Los Angeles, California, Milwaukee, Wisconsin. Another trip to California; Dallas, Texas; trips here in Ohio, all taking much time and preparation for lectures, etc."

Virginia was logging many miles. She was in high demand as a speaker, but also under contract to write more books. Along with her travels, she was "working on a new book for Philomel due in May. But I like being busy."

Virginia discovered a way to balance her travels to speaking engagements and writing commitments. She got rid of her old typewriter.

Virginia embraced technology and, in another letter to Noriko, she shared that she had a new IBM Displaywriter, a computer, and a printer.

"It saves me much time rewriting, for I do all my rewriting right on the screen in front of me."[10]

Virginia needed to save all the time she could in writing and re-writing her **manuscripts**! Her life as a writer involved visiting schools and libraries, participating in conferences, and receiving recognition. But she and Arnold also took time to get away, to vacation at a very special place.

Virginia wrote to Noriko of this little slice of heaven. "We are all fine here. I send you a few pictures of us on our vacation in Puerto Rico—actually, we are in the pictures on the island of Culebra 50 miles east of

VIRGINIA AT HOME, AT WORK ON HER COMPUTER

PR out in the Caribbean. The picture of the water and hills shows the house we have built."

"We bought a strip of land on a bay as you sailed into the small harbor . . . and built our rustic house on a platform . . . along with **cistern** and pump for drinking water. When there was a bit of drought before a visit, you would see me in my little wooden boat washing pots in the middle of the bay using salt water."[11]

Arnold recalled that their getaway home on Culebra involved hard work and great fun. "There were many years when we came down with the kids and suitcases of research materials for whatever book we were working on. First typewriters, then word processors," he shared.[12]

All of the demands were difficult at times. Virginia confided to Noriko in early January 1984 of her challenges in balancing her life as a successful writer.

"I am working on two books. Very difficult. I am always behind and I worry a lot about it. Maybe this year I was too successful. Winning prizes, I had to spend time writing and making speeches, traveling. It is good, though to have everyone like your work. I get such wonderful letters from people. It makes me feel very good."[13]

One of those books she was working on was titled *The People Could Fly: American Black Folktales*. Virginia retold folktales passed down for generations in black families. And as Virginia would share, the storytellers were American, first, and black, second. Virginia's retelling of the tales is beautifully illustrated by Leo and Diane Dillon, who had become good friends of Virginia and Arnold.

The title story is about people of Africa who had the power to fly. Once they were captured for slavery, they had to shed their wings. But they kept their power. And eventually they were able to fly to freedom.

Virginia continued to fly herself, both literally and figuratively. Every new book brought new opportunities for speeches, presentations, and awards. Typically, Virginia and Arnold traveled together, for she didn't care to take trips without him. Often, they were recognized together for their contributions to the world of books for children.

They appeared together at book fairs, promoting their books.

And occasionally they spoke together on panels, having a grand time.

"We were very funny, playing off one another, and they all loved it. We tell the difference between a poet and a prose writer," Virginia said.[14]

They even both taught at Queens College in New York City together.

VIRGINIA MEETS WITH FANS AT THE GREENE COUNTY PUBLIC LIBRARY

One opportunity was a little closer to home. In 1988 Virginia taught at the Ohio State University as a University Distinguished Visiting Professor.

The demands for her books continued. Virginia signed a long-term contract with Harcourt Brace Jovanovich for nine books in 1991.

All of this creativity in her writing and sharing of her wisdom led to a very special recognition in Berlin, Germany, in 1992.

Every other year the International Board on Books for Young People (IBBY) recognizes a living author and an illustrator whose works have made a significant contribution to children's literature.

VIRGINIA AND ARNOLD RECEIVE RECOGNITION FROM
THE BOLINGA BLACK CULTURAL RESOURCES CENTER,
WRIGHT STATE UNIVERSITY, OHIO

VIRGINIA AND ARNOLD AT ONE OF THE MANY BOOK FAIRS
THEY ATTENDED, PROMOTING THEIR BOOKS

© 2016 The Arnold Adoff Revocable Living Trust

The Hans Christian Andersen Award is the highest international recognition given to a children's book author or illustrator.

The Hans Christian Andersen Award is comparable to the **Nobel** prize!

Virginia traveled to Berlin to accept the recognition.

She had with her a little journal, the outside of which resembled a jaguar's sleek coat. The jaguar was her favorite animal. Just as if the journal were a diary, in its inside cover, Virginia wrote, "Property

VIRGINIA AND ARNOLD PRESENTING ON A PANEL DISCUSSION TOGETHER

of V. Hamilton, Her Eyes Only. Enter by special permission." Virginia made notes about the long flight to Berlin, and the seven-hour time difference. She wrote about eating too much and that she "promised to mend my ways starting tomorrow." She wrote on September 3 that the ceremonies for the Andersen Awards were "quite something."[15]

As she typically did for the many awards she received for her work throughout the years, Virginia prepared a speech.

"My life would be perfect if I didn't have to give speeches. I <u>hate</u> speaking! (smile) But I love writing and I suppose people wanting to hear me speak goes with the territory."[16]

Her speeches reflect her gratitude for her writing mentors, editors, and publishers; her husband, Arnold; and her children. Virginia was always gracious in her appreciation to the organization from which she was receiving an award. She often shared her impressions of the host city in her presentation. And, of course, she told stories.

Her prepared comments for the Hans Christian Andersen Award included all of these elements. She noted that she appreciated "your beautiful city, your museums, and your historic monuments. I congratulate you on the tumbling down of walls and on the preservation of democratic ideals."[17]

The famous Berlin Wall had toppled just three years prior, on November 9, 1989. The Wall was constructed in 1961 by the **Communist** government of East Germany. The official purpose of the wall was to keep Western "**fascists**" from going to East Germany to attempt to undermine the government. In reality, the Wall was built to keep those Germans who lived under Communist control from fleeing to West Germany.

The Wall fell when the head of the Communist party announced that citizens could cross the border any time they wanted. Celebrations commenced, as citizens brought hammers and picks and destroyed the structure.

In her speech for the Hans Christian Andersen Award, Virginia reflected on her writing. She offered, "Indeed, it is often said that we authors write especially for children because our childhoods were so vital and heartfelt that we cannot let go of them, ever. But I do write about childhood awareness out of my rich, country experience. I truly loved being a child. I still keep inside me that curious six-year-old, that ten-year-old lover of pranks and jokes, and the defiant thirteen-to-fourteen-year-old."[18]

Virginia continued to embrace and share her love of her childhood until she could share no more.

CAUTION: YOU ARE LEAVING NOW WEST BERLIN

Courtesy National Archives, photo no. 306-BN-104-3(H-32583)

CHILDREN AND THE COLD WAR

AFTER WORLD WAR II Germany was a country divided, as was its capital, Berlin. The Soviet Union controlled part of both Germany and Berlin. The United States and its allies, France and Britain, controlled the rest. The Soviet Union blockaded Berlin in 1948. The Communists would not allow any products to come into Berlin. America responded with the "Berlin Airlift," providing many tons of supplies. American pilots even dropped candy to the children of Berlin. In 1961 the Communists constructed a wall so that East Germans could no longer travel to the free West Germany. Even children were separated from their playmates by the Wall.

DID YOU KNOW?

Vittles, a boxer, was owned by First Lieutenant Clarence
"Russ" Steber. Vittles flew over two thousand hours during
the Berlin Airlift. He even had his own parachute made for
him![19]

CHAPTER TEN

CONCLUSION

For children, reading is the discovery of new worlds of color and texture. For me, writing for children is the creation of worlds of darkness and light. There is an essential line between us, a line of thought and ultimately of communication. Each book must speak, "This is what I have to say," in the hope that each reader will answer, "That is what I wanted to know."[1]

N A LETTER dated March 10, 1991, to Stephanie Spinner, an associate publisher at Knopf, Virginia wrote, "Son Jaime is in California doing a demo; daughter Leigh is in Lyon, Fr., doing auditions. And I would rather be with either one of them than at my desk doing THIS."[1]

THIS was editing her manuscript, *Many Thousand Gone: African Americans from Slavery to Freedom,* one of the few nonfiction works that Virginia wrote. The book features a collection of stories from the plantation era in America. Illustrations, placed throughout the book, were created by Leo and Diane Dillon.

For all of her time involved in imagining, remembering, and creating her stories, Virginia always made time for her children. She likely would have preferred to spend more time with them than in writing and rewriting her stories.

"What I remember so vividly is that when I wanted to run track *and* play in the orchestra, the school thought it was too much and I

VIRGINIA, JAIME, LEIGH, AND ARNOLD AT HOME IN 1982

should pick just one. But I didn't pick just one, and Mom drove me to every meet and concert. She would bring my track spikes and concert gown and violin in our old Gran Torino station wagon, and I would change in the "way back" as she drove me to the next venue, so to speak," Leigh said.[2]

Leigh went on to follow one of those passions, one that had always been present in their home—music. Leigh is an accomplished soprano, performing in many European opera and concert halls.

Jaime also pursued a musical career. But, after a while, he decided to leave the music business behind. He called home to deliver the news.

"The phone rang. Virginia answered it. Virginia *never* answered the phone. It was Jaime," Arnold shared. "He told Virginia he was coming home and joining the family business."

"And what business would that be?" Virginia asked, a slight smile on her face.[3]

Jaime became a children's book author. Then, after several successful titles, he chose to go in a different direction in the family business. He teaches young people.

Virginia was a writer throughout her life. But she was also a teacher. She taught young people that there are worlds to imagine beyond your own. She taught readers that you can remember where you grew up and share your stories from your experiences. She taught writers that, using your imagination and all that you remember and know, you can create stories that are uniquely yours.

"The **multiplicity** of themes, the details of each of the threads throughout her stories, the demands she made of her young readers, no one has been able to emulate that since in children's literature," Arnold said.[4]

Her friend Rudine Sims Bishop, **professor emerita** of education at the Ohio State University, shared, "I think she opened the door for today's authors to mine their own family history and their group history and their cultural traditions for stories—both fiction and nonfiction.[5]

"Virginia often wrote about slavery and its effects in that era, people who had been enslaved. She talked about Liberation Literature as allowing the reader to be a witness to the protagonist's suffering and also the triumph. Both the protagonist in the story and the reader are therefore liberated, thus Liberation Literature."[6]

Professor Bishop also offered when asked how they became friends, "I was a fan of Virginia's. To me she was like a rock star. So I worked to get other people to recognize how great she was. I successfully lobbied to have her appointed Visiting Distinguished Professor at Ohio State, and sat in on the classes she taught. I also successfully nominated her to receive an honorary degree from Ohio State."

"One year I got to ride with her and her husband to the Virginia Hamilton Conference at Kent State. She drove a big white Jaguar! Quite a luxury."[7]

MACARTHUR FELLOWSHIP

THE "GENIUS GRANT" is an "unrestricted fellowship to talented individuals who have shown extraordinary originality and dedication in their creative pursuits and a marked capacity for self-direction."[8]

In other words, the MacArthur Foundation offers money to encourage creativity. On the MacArthur Foundation website, this is what was written about Virginia: "Hamilton did not create a **saccharine,** fluffy, or **pristine** literary world for children. She respected their intelligence and their abilities to grapple with ideas."

Virginia continued to balance her personal life with all the demands of her career as a highly honored children's book author.

The honors extended to Virginia included the MacArthur Fellowship, otherwise known as the "Genius Grant," in 1995. Virginia was the first children's book writer to receive this award!

That same year, Virginia was awarded the Laura Ingalls Wilder Award. This award, named after the creator of the classic *Little House on the Prairie* series, is given each year to the author or illustrator of books published in the United States who has, over his or her lifetime, made a significant contribution to children's literature.

At a conference in Cambridge, England, titled "Travelers in Time: Past, Present, and to Come," Virginia became quite reflective in her remarks.

"What does happen to time in a book? Whose time is there in a book? What happens to the writer's time; what is its significance, its definition?"[9]

Perhaps Virginia had a premonition that time was slipping away from her. Just several years later she discovered she had cancer.

VIRGINIA AND ARNOLD CELEBRATING NEW YEAR'S EVE AT
HOME, 1984

"After July, I began to sleep, sleep, sleep and I became ill. Very rare for me to be ill. But I was in the hospital to have a cyst removed from my sternum," Virginia wrote to her friend, Noriko Shima, in September 1994.

She fought valiantly and quietly for nearly ten years. Sadly, her story came to an end entirely too soon. Virginia died on February 19, 2002.

In her memorial-service booklet, Arnold wrote, "Dylan was wrong. Of course Death has Dominion Over All. But Finest Work Prevails Through Generations . . ."

Virginia may have left this world, but she left so much to remember her by.

VIRGINIA AND HER SIBLINGS DURING A FAMILY REUNION.
FROM LEFT: BUSTER, VIRGINIA, BARBARA, NINA, AND BILLY

She left behind a family who loved her dearly.

She left behind a wealth of friends both in and out of the literary world who were heartbroken by her passing. She is remembered fondly by many, including her friend Nikki Giovanni, an award-winning poet and university distinguished professor at Virginia Tech.

"I recruited my friend Barb to help me start the first Cincinnati Black Arts Festival. We rounded up the kids and created things that they could do. I had just recently read *Zeely* by Virginia, and I, along with the rest of the world, fell in love with it. I thought a play from the book would be a marvelous thing so I wrote it.

"The Arts Festival was, luckily, written up in both the local Black newspaper and the *Cincinnati Enquirer.* It received positive reviews and

VIRGINIA SAILING
ON THE *QUEEN
ELIZABETH 2*, 2000

VIRGINIA AND ARNOLD OUTSIDE THEIR HOME IN YELLOW SPRINGS

© 2016 The Arnold Adoff Revocable Living Trust

we were thrilled. I did, however, get a letter from Virginia Hamilton asking to meet me. I had no idea that I had done anything wrong. She lived in Yellow Springs and Barb and I drove up one evening to meet her. She wondered where I got permission to make *Zeely* a play. It took me a minute to understand I had committed an infraction. I apologized profusely and asked how I could make it up. Virginia, or Ginny, as we learned to call her, laughed and said it was all right.

"I always remembered her generosity and we saw each other from time to time when I was in Cincinnati. I was and remain a big fan of her work. I am sorry that she is now writing for all the good boys and girls in heaven."[10]

Jerry Pinkney has illustrated over one hundred books since he began doing so in 1964. He has won many major awards for his work, including the Caldecott Medal, given every year to the illustrator of the

JAIME READS FROM HIS EARLY COPY OF HIS FIRST CHILDREN'S BOOK WHILE ARNOLD PROUDLY LOOKS ON. THE PHOTOGRAPH WAS TAKEN AT THE VIRGINIA HAMILTON CONFERENCE IN 2002, JUST MONTHS AFTER VIRGINIA DIED

most distinguished children's book. Jerry's beautiful works have received Caldecott Honors five times, as well as five Coretta Scott King Awards. He was the United States' nominee for the Hans Christian Andersen Award in 1998.

Jerry also illustrated several of Virginia's books, including *Jahdu* and *Drylongso*. He received the Virginia Hamilton Literary Award in 2000.

"Without question, Virginia Hamilton's work remains some of the most influential by a picture-book or young-adult writer to date. With a deep passion for her roots, Hamilton's text captures the magic of oral storytelling of times past while projecting her understanding of culture into the future. I liken her gift of language and imagination to Toni Morrison's: lyrical, deep, and layered," he shared.[11]

She left behind a collection of frogs. Yes, frogs.

"We always had many little frogs in the fields around our house in Yellow Springs," Arnold said. "Virginia loved them and began to collect frogs as we would travel around the world. We considered them good luck—live, and in various ceramic and carved stone pieces. This end of town used to be called Frogtown, and Virginia thought that might have something to do with her fascination. As the years went on, people would give us frogs as gifts and we continued to collect until her death."[12]

She left behind the legacy of the Virginia Hamilton Conference and inspiration for those who continue to carry the torch in organizing the annual event celebrating and encouraging multicultural literature for children.

Conference co-director Alexa Sandmann remembers Virginia in this way, "Her presence was warm, but very regal."

Ashley Bryan, who received the Virginia Hamilton Literary Award in 2003 as well as the Coretta Scott King–Virginia Hamilton Award for Lifetime Achievement in 2012, shared his thoughts about Virginia.

He wrote, "It is a joy that Virginia Hamilton lives on through her glorious books and the conference in her name."

He continued, "Virginia is especially alive during her annual conference. Still, I always remember her warm reception and recognition of others. I hear her rich tone of voice in her readings and song. Her outreach to audiences dramatized her dedication and commitment to her art."

And finally Bryan noted, "Virginia's presence alone, her regal bearing, stirred others to a realization of their gifts. This is the reality of the loving human being she was. This keeps Virginia ever alive in me."[13]

The fireflies still dance above the fields near Virginia's home in Yellow Springs every summer. They remind us, just like Virginia's immortal words spoken by her character Mr. Pool in *The Planet of Junior Brown*, "This life holds wonders for us all."[14]

Virginia's stories *are* filled with wonder. And just like those fireflies in the summer, her stories are always there, just waiting for us to capture their magic.

Virginia may be gone from this world, but her life's work continues to inspire children's book authors and illustrators. Her amazing storytelling abilities, encouraged from when she was that little girl sitting on her father's lap, continue to entertain readers of all ages. And her legacy of being America's most honored children's book author, ever, remains.

Perhaps Zeely, her character from her break-out novel, sums up Virginia best: "She was the days and nights put together."[15]

DID YOU KNOW?

If you visit www.virginiahamilton.com, and click on the frog, you'll find the answer to this joke:
    What did the frog order at McDonald's?

OHIO HISTORICAL MARKER DEDICATED TO VIRGINIA HAMILTON, MARCH 2017, AT THE YELLOW SPRINGS COMMUNITY LIBRARY

Ohio History Connection

Virginia's Timeline

THE FOLLOWING represents the highlights of Virginia's life and writing career. A full listing of Virginia's works can be found under the complete chronological list of her works. In addition, a separate record of the most notable of Virginia's honors follows in the awards and recognition chapter. Please note that recognition attributed to her works reflects the year the work was published.

1934   *March 12:* Virginia Perry Hamilton is born in Yellow Springs, Ohio.

1953   *September:* Virginia receives a scholarship to attend Antioch College in Yellow Springs.

1956   Virginia transfers to the Ohio State University, majoring in literature and creative writing.

        Virginia moves to New York City.

1960   *March 19:* Virginia marries Arnold Adoff in New York City.

1963   Leigh Hamilton Adoff is born.

1967   Jaime Levi Adoff is born.

1967   Virginia's first book, *Zeely,* is published. *Zeely* is named an American Library Association Notable Book.

1968   *The House of Dies Drear* receives the Edgar Allan Poe Award, "The Edgar."

1969   Virginia, Arnold, Leigh, and Jaime move back to Yellow Springs, Ohio.

1975   Virginia wins the Newbery Medal for her book *M.C. Higgins, the Great.* She is the first African American to receive this honor. In addition, *M.C. Higgins, the Great* receives the National Book Award and the Boston Globe–Horn Book Award, becoming the first book to receive all three prestigious awards.

1979   Virginia is a delegate to the Second International Conference of Writers for Children and Youth in Moscow.

1982	Virginia's book *Sweet Whispers, Brother Rush* wins numerous awards, including the Coretta Scott King Award, Boston Globe–Horn Book Award, and an IBBY Honor Book Citation, and is named a Newbery Honor Book and an American Book Awards Honor Book.
1985	*April 12:* The first Virginia Hamilton Lectureship on Minority Group Experiences in Children's Literature (now known simply as the Virginia Hamilton Conference) is held at Kent State University.
1987	Virginia and Arnold are named distinguished visiting professors at Queens College in New York.
1989	Virginia is named distinguished writing professor, Graduate School of Education, Ohio State University.
1992	Virginia travels to Berlin to accept the Hans Christian Andersen Author Award. The Andersen Award is the highest international recognition bestowed on an author or illustrator of children's literature, and has been given to one author and one illustrator every other year since 1956. Virginia is only the fourth American to win the writing award, and one of just six Americans who have won either Andersen Award.
1993	Virginia speaks at the Pacific Rim Conference on Children's Literature in Kyoto, Japan. This conference was organized by Virginia's dear friend Noriko Shima.
1995	Virginia becomes the first children's book author ever to win a MacArthur Fellowship. This distinction is nicknamed the "Genius Grant."
1995	Virginia is awarded the Laura Ingalls Wilder Award for her "substantial and lasting contribution to literature for children."
2001	Virginia is awarded the de Grummond Award Medal for lifetime achievement in children's literature from the University of Southern Mississippi. Her acceptance is Virginia's last public speech. It also marks the first and only time that she appears professionally with her son, Jaime Adoff.
2002	*February 19:* Virginia dies of breast cancer.

Three of Virginia's works were published after her death: *Time Pieces, Bruh Rabbit and the Tar Baby Girl,* and *Wee Winnie Witch's Skinny.*

Virginia's Awards and Recognition

In alphabetical order

VIRGINIA HAMILTON was one of the most distinguished authors of twentieth-century youth literature. She received nearly every award in the field during her thirty-five-year career, including:

American Book Awards Honor Book (*Sweet Whispers, Brother Rush*)

Arbuthnot Honor Lecture (American Library Association), 1993

Blackboard African American Bestsellers Winner (*Her Stories*), 1996

Boston Globe–Horn Book Award for Fiction (*Sweet Whispers, Brother Rush; M. C. Higgins, the Great*) and for Nonfiction (*Anthony Burns*)

Coretta Scott King Award (*The People Could Fly; Sweet Whispers, Brother Rush; Her Stories*) and Honor Book Award (*Anthony Burns; The Magical Adventures of Pretty Pearl; The Bells of Christmas*)

de Grummond Medal from the University of Southern Mississippi, 2001

Edgar Allan Poe Award ("The Edgar") from the Mystery Writers of America (*The House of Dies Drear*)

The Educational Press Association of America Distinguished Achievement Award, 1997

Hans Christian Andersen Medal, for the body of her work, 1992

International Board on Books for Young People (IBBY) U.S. Honour Book (*M.C. Higgins, the Great*)

International Board on Books for Young People (IBBY) U.S. Honour Book (*Sweet Whispers, Brother Rush*)

Jane Addams Children's Book Award (*Anthony Burns: The Defeat and Triumph of a Fugitive Slave*)

John Newbery Medal (*M.C. Higgins, the Great*) and Honor Book (*Sweet Whispers, Brother Rush; The Planet of Junior Brown; In the Beginning: Creation Stories from Around the World*)

Laura Ingalls Wilder Award, for the body of her work, 1995

Library of Congress Best Books for Children (*Sweet Whispers, Brother Rush*)

MacArthur Fellowship ("Genius Grant"), 1995

The Marquis Who's Who in America, 1996

NAACP Image Award for Outstanding Literary Work for Children (*Her Stories: African American Folktales, Fairy Tales, and True Tales*)

National Book Award (*M.C. Higgins, the Great*)

New York Times Outstanding Children's Book of the Year (*M.C. Higgins, the Great*)

Ohioana Award: Juvenile Literature for Her Body of Work, 1984; Career Medal, 1991; Ohio's Favorite Author of Children's Books, 1999

Ohio Governor's Award, 2000

Ohio Humanities Council, Richard Bjornson Distinguished Service Award, 1993

Ohio Women's Hall of Fame, 1993

Regina Medal of the Catholic Library Association, 1991

Storytelling World Award, 1996 (*Her Stories: African American Folktales, Fairy Tales, and True Tales*)

Time Magazine, One of Twelve Best Books for Young Readers, 1988 (*In the Beginning: Creation Stories from Around the World*)

Virginia Hamilton Conference on Multicultural Literature for Youth, an annual event, is established at Kent State University in 1984 in Hamilton's honor

Appointments, Distinguished Visiting Professor:

Graduate School, Department of Education; Queens College; New York City, New York; 1986–87 and 1987–88

Graduate School, Department of Educational Theory and Practice; Ohio State University; Columbus, Ohio; 1988–89

Honorary Degrees, Doctor of Humane Letters:

  Bank Street College of Education; New York City, New York

  Kent State University; Kent, Ohio

  Ohio State University; Columbus, Ohio

  Wright State University; Dayton, Ohio

Virginia's Chronological List of Works

Based on year of publication*

1967   *Zeely.* Illustrated by Symeon Shimin. New York: Macmillan. In this female initiation story, Geeder Perry and her brother, Toeboy, go to their uncle's farm for the summer and encounter a six-and-a-half-foot-tall Watusi queen and a mysterious night traveler.

1968   *The House of Dies Drear.* Illustrated by Eros Keith. New York: Macmillan. Winner of the Edgar Allan Poe Award. Thomas Small and his family move to the great and forbidding House of Dies Drear, a home that was on the Underground Railroad, and trouble begins.

1969   *The Time-Ago Tales of Jahdu.* Illustrated by Nonny Hogrogian. New York: Macmillan. Four light-hearted tales celebrate the deeds of a "strong black boy," who is a world-class trickster.

1971   *The Planet of Junior Brown.* New York: Macmillan. A Newbery Honor Book. Junior Brown, a three-hundred-pound musical prodigy, plays a piano with no sound while his homeless friend, Buddy Clark, draws on all his wit and New York City resources to protect Junior and save his disintegrating mind.

1972   *W. E. B. Du Bois: A Biography.* New York: Thomas Y. Crowell. This study of the great scholar's life shows how he strove to live up to his enormous potential and to liberate himself from all manner of governmental, political, and societal constraints.

1973   *Time-Ago Lost: More Tales of Jahdu.* Illustrated by Ray Prather. New York: Macmillan. This contains more tales of the world-class trickster.

* From www.virginiahamilton.com

1974   *M.C. Higgins, the Great.* New York: Macmillan. Winner of the John Newbery Medal, the National Book Award, and the Boston Globe–Horn Book Award. Mayo Cornelius Higgins, called M.C., sits atop a forty-foot pole on the side of Sarah's Mountain and dreams of escape. But poised above his home is a massive spoil heap from strip-mining that could come crashing down.

1974   *Paul Robeson: The Life and Times of a Free Black Man.* New York: Harper & Row. The importance of the famous athlete, singer, movie star, and political activist becomes clear in this compelling biography.

1975   *The Writings of W.E. B. Du Bois.* New York: Thomas Y. Crowell. A selection of essays, articles, speeches, and excerpts from writings by W. E. B. Du Bois records his views on a variety of social injustices. Edited by Virginia Hamilton.

1976   *Arilla Sun Down.* New York: Greenwillow Books. This novel of psychic realism follows the story of a biracial family in which the daughter, Arilla, is uncertain of her identity in light of her older brother's overwhelming Amerindian warrior presence.

1978   *Justice and Her Brothers.* New York: Greenwillow Books. The first book of the Justice Trilogy introduces the protagonist, Justice Douglass, her brothers, Thomas and Levi, and a friend, Dorian. In these novels, the four mind-jump to a future Earth a million years from today, only to find a wasteland controlled by an entity known as Mal.

1980   *Dustland.* New York: Greenwillow Books. This is the second book of the Justice Trilogy.

1980   *Jahdu.* Illustrated by Jerry Pinkney. New York: Greenwillow Books. This continues the *Jahdu* saga with more tales of the grand trickster.

1981   *The Gathering.* New York: Greenwillow Books. This book concludes the Justice Trilogy.

1982   *Sweet Whispers, Brother Rush.* New York: Philomel Books. A Newbery Honor Book and winner of the Boston Globe–Horn Book Award and the Coretta Scott King Award. This novel, which confronts issues of child abuse, single-parent families, and the death of a young person, turns on the appearances and disappearances of a ghost, Brother Rush.

1983 *The Magical Adventures of Pretty Pearl.* New York: HarperCollins. This fantasy—part myth, part legend and folklore—tells the story of Pretty Pearl. When she comes down from the God home of Mount Kenya to live among real people, Pearl discovers the diaspora of the slave trade and forgets all her brother god's warnings about being true to the goddess within her.

1983 *Willie Bea and the Time the Martians Landed.* New York: Greenwillow Books. This old-fashioned, humorous novel tells about the night in October 1938 when Orson Welles broadcast his famous radio adaptation of H. G. Wells's tale of a Martian invasion of Earth and scared legions of Americans who believed the invasion was really happening.

1984 *A Little Love.* New York: Philomel Books. Sheema Hadley searches for the father she never knew, who never wanted to know her, and ultimately finds new strength in herself.

1985 *Junius Over Far.* New York: HarperCollins. This cross-cultural adventure takes place in America and the Caribbean.

1985 *The People Could Fly: American Black Folktales.* Illustrated by Leo and Diane Dillon. New York: Knopf. Distributed by Random House. Winner of the Coretta Scott King Award. These twenty-four tales present a significant body of black folklore and bring us closer to the hearts and minds of the people who first told them and passed them on to us.

1987 *The Mystery of Drear House.* New York: Greenwillow Books. This concludes the Dies Drear Chronicle.

1987 *A White Romance.* New York: Philomel Books. This timely coming-of-age novel, with sex, drugs, and rock and roll, has a none-too-subtle biracial theme.

1988   *Anthony Burns: The Defeat and Triumph of a Fugitive Slave.* New York: Knopf. Winner of the Boston Globe–Horn Book Award. A historical reconstruction of a poor man's life, told against the backdrop of the Civil War, focuses on the struggles of this common man.

1988   *In the Beginning: Creation Stories from Around the World.* Illustrated by Barry Moser. San Diego: Harcourt. A Newbery Honor Book. Twenty-five stories from cultures around the globe explain the creation of people and the universe.

1989   *The Bells of Christmas.* Illustrated by Lambert Davis. San Diego: Harcourt. An ALA Notable Book. A traditional story about the members of a prosperous African American family in Ohio narrates their celebration of Christmas.

1990   *Cousins.* New York: Philomel Books. Three cousins set out on an emotional journey one summer, during which rivalry and deep hostility develop, and a death occurs.

1990   *The Dark Way: Stories from the Spirit World.* Illustrated by Lambert Davis. San Diego: Harcourt. This illustrated collection tells compelling multiethnic and multicultural scare tales from around the world.

1991   *The All Jahdu Storybook.* Illustrated by Barry Moser. San Diego: Harcourt. This illustrated revision of Hamilton's *Jahdu* saga rolls all of the three books of tales into one.

1992   *Drylongso.* Illustrated by Jerry Pinkney. San Diego: Harcourt. A family struggling against forces of nature—weather, climate, and a huge dust storm—meets a stranger named Drylongso, who, with his divining rod, finds a life-giving underground spring.

1993   *Many Thousand Gone: African Americans from Slavery to Freedom.* Illustrated by Leo and Diane Dillon. New York: Knopf. Distributed by Random House. These nonfiction stories about the plantation era in America include factual slave-escape accounts and portraits of real people in their historical context.

1993 *Plain City.* New York: Blue Sky Press. In the stillness of winter, Buhlaire Sims is ready to get some answers about her family in this coming-of-age novel about people of various colors and classes.

1995 *Her Stories: African American Folktales, Fairy Tales, and True Tales.* Illustrated by Leo and Diane Dillon. New York: Blue Sky Press. Winner of the Coretta Scott King Award. This collection features female protagonists and spans generations, from girl child to elder woman, with stories ranging from a Cinderella-type fantasy to long-ago folktales and true narratives of real women.

1995 *Jaguarundi.* Illustrated by Floyd Cooper. New York: Blue Sky Press. Endangered animals must make their way to freedom in this original picture-book story.

1996 *When Birds Could Talk & Bats Could Sing: The Adventures of Bruh Sparrow, Sis Wren, and Their Friends.* Illustrated by Barry Moser. New York: Blue Sky Press. A wonderfully humorous collection of bird tales retells stories from plantation-era slaves in colloquial, or everyday, speech.

1997 *A Ring of Tricksters: Animal Tales from America, the West Indies, and Africa.* Illustrated by Barry Moser. New York: Blue Sky Press. This presents eleven of the best animal-trickster tales ever, gathered from the storytelling ring of the slave trade during the American plantation era.

1998 *Second Cousins.* New York: Blue Sky Press. In this sequel to *Cousins,* a family reunion brings two sophisticated second cousins from New York City—setting Cammy's world off balance.

1999 *Bluish: A Novel.* New York: Blue Sky Press. A new girl arrives at school in a wheelchair, and some of the children call her "Bluish." Her leukemia makes her seem different, but Dreenie's overwhelming curiosity leads her and another student, Tuli, to reach beyond their fear.

2000 *The Girl Who Spun Gold.* Illustrated by Leo and Diane Dillon. New York: Blue Sky Press. This stunning picture-book folktale retells the classic fairytale "Rumpelstiltskin," in which a girl must spin gold for a king or die. In this West Indian-based story, Quashiba must guess the name of her magical helper, Lit'mahn Bittyun.

2001   *Time Pieces: The Book of Times.* New York: Blue Sky Press. Hamilton's semiautobiographical novel weaves together the present time and slave times. Published posthumously.

2003   *Bruh Rabbit and the Tar Baby Girl.* Illustrated by James Ransome. New York: Blue Sky Press. Hamilton adds her magic to a popular African American story and tells it in authentic colloquial speech. Published posthumously.

2004   *Wee Winnie Witch's Skinny: An Original African American Scare Tale.* Illustrated by Barry Moser. New York: Blue Sky Press. A wild night ride of bewitchment and fright is based on an 1800s African American scary tale about a woman who outwits a witch and steals her skin. Published posthumously.

2010   *Virginia Hamilton: Speeches, Essays, and Conversations.* Edited by Arnold Adoff and Kacy Cook. New York: Blue Sky Press.

Glossary

Abolitionist: A person who believes in the end of a practice or institution, such as slavery

Appeal: To be attractive or interesting

Apprehend: To catch a criminal or suspect

Araucanas: A breed of chicken that originated in Chile, known for its blue eggs

Bohemian: A person or place with informal or unconventional social habits

Candor: The quality of being open and honest

Cistern: A tank for storing water

Communist: A person who believes in, or a government based on, a political theory that supports a society in which all property is publicly owned and each person works and is paid according to their abilities and needs

Conflict: An incompatibility between two or more opinions, principles, or interests

Correspondence: Letters sent or received

Coveted: Highly desirable

Deliberation: Careful and long consideration or discussion

Entranced: Filled with wonder, focused entirely on someone or something

Fascists: Followers of an authoritarian and nationalistic right-wing system of government; those who tend to believe in the supremacy of one national or ethnic group

Genre: A category of artistic composition as in music or literature

Gigs: Live performances of a musician

Idolize: Admire excessively

Ingenuity: Quality of being clever and original

Intervene: To come between two or more sides in order to change a course of events

Keynote: The main theme at a conference, typically addressed by the primary speaker

Kremlin: The Russian (formerly USSR) government housed within the citadel of the same name

Lectern: A tall stand with a sloped top to hold notes for a lecturer

Legislature: The legislative, or lawmaking, body of a country or state

Letterhead: A person's or company's stationery with a printed heading stating the name and address

Mainstream: Ideas or attitudes that are considered normal

Mandolin: A musical instrument, resembling a lute, with paired metal strings plucked with a pick

Manuscripts: An author's texts that have not yet been published

Marinara: A sauce made from tomatoes, onions, and herbs

Miscegenation: Marriage or cohabitation of two people from different racial groups

Momentous: Of great importance or significance

Multiplicity: A large number or variety

Nobel: Any of six international awards given every year for outstanding work in chemistry, economics, literature, physics, physiology or medicine, and the promotion of peace

Patriarch: The male head of a family

Persona: The aspect of someone's personality that is seen by others

Pristine: Perfect, spotless, flawless

Prodigy: A young person with exceptional abilities or talents

Professor emerita: A distinguished retired female professor

Protagonist: A major character in a novel

Red Square: A large square in Moscow next to the Kremlin

Repeal: To revoke or annul a law or congressional act

Resplendent: Beautiful, stunning; attractive and impressive

Saccharine: Excessively sweet

Socialism: A political and economic theory that believes in the community overseeing the production, distribution, and exchange of goods

Suspend: To temporarily stop from occurring or being in force or effect

Transition: The adjustment from one state to another

Traverse: To travel across

Underground Railroad: A secret network for helping slaves escape from the South to the North and to Canada in the years before the Civil War

Unnerve: To make someone lose confidence, discompose, fluster

Venture: To dare to do something or go somewhere that may be dangerous or unpleasant

Acknowledgments

I AM SO honored by the assistance and support of many individuals in my journey to research and share the life of Virginia Hamilton.

First and foremost is my husband Brad and our children, Kyle and Ian. Love you to the moon and back! And, as always, this is in honor and memory of Claire.

Arnold Adoff was an amazing resource at the start and a friend in the end.

The staff at Ohio University Press has been amazing to work with. My thanks go to Gillian Berchowitz, Rick Huard, Samara Rafert, Jeff Kallet, Maryann Gunderson, and all the other team members who believe in me and my ability to share Virginia's lifework and journey. My work would not be nearly as precise without the editorial input of Nancy Basmajian and Chiquita Babb.

The following individuals were helpful specifically in uncovering the many layers of Virginia:

The staff at the Library of Congress.

Scott Sanders, Antioch College Archivist.

Alexa Sandmann and Sarah M. Harper, for meeting with me and offering input on the Virginia Hamilton Conference.

Amanda Faehnel and the staff at the Kent State Libraries, Special Collections and Archives.

Carrie Bertram and the staff at the American Library Association.

Leslee Hooper of the Toledo Lucas County Public Library.

Connie Collette of the Greene County Public Library.

A huge thank you goes to Virginia's friends in the literary world who were willing to share their memories, including Rudine Sims Bishop, Ashley Bryan, Nikki Giovanni, Angela Johnson, Jerry Pinkney, and Noriko Shima.

I am so grateful to my early readers for guiding Virginia's life story into the narrative it has become. They include Linda Hoetzl, Amy Zavac, Kyle, and Brad. I am indebted to Brandon Marie Miller, an awesome nonfiction author, for her incredible guidance and input.

Most of all, thank you, Virginia, for your amazing life.

It has been my honor to share your story.

Notes

Chapter One: Characters

*Virginia Hamilton, "Coretta Scott King Award Acceptance Speech: *Sweet Whispers, Brother Rush*" (American Library Conference, 1983). From *Speeches, Essays, and Conversations*, ed. Arnold Adoff and Kacy Cook (New York: Blue Sky Press, 2010), 111.

1. Virginia Hamilton, "AH, Sweet Rememory," *Horn Book Magazine*. From *Speeches, Essays, and Conversations*, 94.

2. Nina Mikkelsen, *Virginia Hamilton* (New York: Twayne, 1994), 4.

3. Ibid.

4. Rudine Sims Bishop, "Virginia Hamilton," *Horn Book Magazine* 71, no. 4 (July/August 1995): 442.

5. Mikkelsen, *Virginia Hamilton*, 5.

6. Hamilton, "AH, Sweet Rememory," 98.

7. Virginia Hamilton, "Illusions and Reality" (lecture, Library of Congress, Washington DC, November 17, 1975). From *Speeches, Essays, and Conversations*, 56.

8. Virginia Hamilton, "Coretta Scott King Award Acceptance Speech: *The People Could Fly: American Black Folktales*" (American Library Association, New York City, 1986). From *Speeches, Essays, and Conversations*, 133.

9. Virginia Hamilton, "The Knowledge" (essay). In *Paul Robeson: The Life and Times of a Free Black Man* (New York: Harper & Row, 1974), xv.

10. Virginia Hamilton, "Reflections" (The Marygrove College Contemporary American Authors Lecture, April 1997, Detroit, MI). From *Speeches, Essays, and Conversations*, 286.

11. Virginia Hamilton website, www.virginiahamilton.com.

12. Virginia Hamilton, "Sentinels in Long Still Rows," *American Libraries* 30, no. 6 (June/July, 1999): 68.

13. Virginia Hamilton website.

14. Virginia Hamilton, *Her Stories: African American Folk Tales, Fairy Tales, and True Tales* (New York: Blue Sky Press, 1995), 107.

15. Ibid., 106.

16. Virginia Hamilton website, The Past.

17. Hamilton, "Coretta Scott King Award Acceptance Speech: *The People Could Fly: American Black Folktales*," From *Speeches, Essays, and Conversations*, 111.

18. Sims Bishop, "Virginia Hamilton," 442.

19. Mikkelsen, *Virginia Hamilton*, 3.

20. Judy Petsonk, "Writer Harnesses Powerful Prose with Discipline," *Dayton Daily News*, May 16, 1976, 20.

21. Ibid.

22. Virginia Hamilton, "Newbery Acceptance Speech: *M.C. Higgins, the Great*" (American Library Association, 1975). From *Speeches, Essays, and Conversations*, 45.

23. Virginia Hamilton, "Literature, Creativity, and Imagination" (lecture, George Peabody College for Teachers, Nashville, TN, 1972). From *Speeches, Essays, and Conversations*, 29–30.

24. Virginia Hamilton, *The House of Dies Drear* (New York: Macmillan, 1968), 247.

25. Virginia Hamilton website, A Virginia Rememory.

26. Bruce Chadwick, *Traveling the Underground Railroad* (Secaucus, NJ: Carol Publishing Group, 1999), 3.

27. Dennis Brindell Fradin, *Bound for the North Star: True Stories of Fugitive Slaves* (New York: Clarion Books, 2000), 33.

Chapter Two: Setting

*Virginia Hamilton, "Changing Woman, Working" (essay). In *Celebrating Children's Books: Essays on Children's Literature in honor of Zena Sutherland*. From *Speeches, Essays, and Conversations*, 103.

1. Mikkelsen, *Virginia Hamilton*, 5.

2. Hamilton, "Sentinels in Long Still Rows," 68.

3. Ibid., 68.

4. Ibid., 68.

5. Hamilton, "The Knowledge," xi.

6. Frank Quillin, *The Color Line in Ohio: A History of Race Prejudice in a Typical Northern State* (Ann Arbor: University of Michigan Press, 1913), 21.

7. Stephen Middleton, *The Black Laws: Race and the Legal Process in Early Ohio* (Athens: Ohio University Press, 2005), 4.

8. Diane Chiddister, "A History of Racial Diversity," *Yellow Springs News* (Yellow Springs, OH), February 10, 2010.

9. *Two Hundred Years of Yellow Springs: A Collection of Articles First Published in the* Yellow Springs News *for the 2003 Bicentennial of Yellow Springs, Ohio* (Yellow Springs, OH: Yellow Springs News), 138.

10. Robert H. Mayer, *When the Children Marched: The Birmingham Civil Rights Movement* (Berkeley Heights, NJ: Enslow, 2008), 117.

11. Mikkelsen, *Virginia Hamilton*, 6.

Chapter Three: Plot Twist

*Mikkelsen, *Virginia Hamilton*, 6.

1. Interview with Arnold Adoff, June 5, 2015.

2. Mikkelsen, *Virginia Hamilton*, 7.

3. Ibid., 6.

4. Virginia Hamilton, "Portrait of the Author as a Working Writer," *Elementary English*, an official publication of the National Council of Teachers of English, April 1971. From *Speeches, Essays, and Conversations*, 18.

5. Interview with Arnold Adoff, June 5, 2015.

6. Virginia Hamilton, "Planting Seeds," *Horn Book Magazine* 68, no. 6 (November 1992): 674.

7. Phone interview with Arnold Adoff, October 27, 2015.

8. Interview with Arnold Adoff, June 5, 2015.

9. Phone interview with Arnold Adoff, October 27, 2015.

10. Ibid.

11. Interview with Arnold Adoff, June 5, 2015.

12. Mikkelsen, *Virginia Hamilton*, 7.

13. Interview with Arnold Adoff, June 5, 2015.

14. Scholastic Publishers website, www.scholastic.com/teachers/articles/teaching content/virginia-hamilton-interview-transcript/.

Chapter Four: Voice

*Rudine Sims Bishop, "Books from Parallel Cultures: Celebrating a Silver Anniversary," *Horn Book Magazine* 69, no. 2 (March/April 1993): 175.

1. Virginia Hamilton, *Zeely* (New York: Macmillan, 1967), 114.

2. Interview with Arnold Adoff, June 4, 2015.

3. Interview with Arnold Adoff, September 15, 2015.

4. Phone interview with Arnold Adoff, October 28, 2015.

5. Ibid.

6. Email correspondence with Arnold Adoff, November 5, 2015.

7. Ibid.

8. Mikkelsen, *Virginia Hamilton*, 8.

9. Susan Dudley Gold, *Loving v. Virginia: Lifting the Ban against Interracial Marriage* (Tarrytown, NY: Marshall Cavendish Benchmark, 2008), 8–13.

10. Ibid., 107.

Chapter Five: Flashback

*Virginia Hamilton, "Portrait of the Author as a Working Writer," 19.

1. *Two Hundred Years of Yellow Springs*, 159.

2. Hamilton, "Portrait of the Author as a Working Writer," 19.

3. Arnold Adoff, "Arnold: Late at Night in Ginny's Office." From *Speeches, Essays, and Conversations*, 341.

4. Virginia Hamilton to Ellen Rudin, November 15, 1974, Virginia Hamilton Papers, Library of Congress.

5. Don Wallis, "Where's The House of Dies Drear? Virginia Hamilton's Imagination," *Yellow Spring News*, November 21, 1984.

6. Ibid.

7. Virginia Hamilton, *M.C. Higgins, the Great* (New York: Macmillan, 1974), 1–20.

8. Virginia Hamilton, "Coretta Scott King Award Acceptance Speech: *The People Could Fly: American Black Folktales*," 132.

9. Doug McInnis, "Focus: Muskingum County, Ohio: From Strip Mine to African Game Preserve," *New York Times*, June 25, 1989.

10. The Wilds Media Kit, https://columbuszoo.org/home/about/press-releases.

Chapter Six: Turning Point

*Hamilton, "Newbery Acceptance Speech: *M.C. Higgins, the Great*," 51.

1. Hamilton, "Newbery Acceptance Speech: *M.C. Higgins, the Great*," 44.

2. Ibid., 45.

3. Ibid., 47.

4. Phone conversation with Arnold Adoff, January 12, 2016.

5. Hamilton, "Newbery Acceptance Speech: *M.C. Higgins, the Great*," 51.

6. Ibid., 51.

7. Phone interview with Arnold Adoff, July 29, 2016.

Chapter Seven: Flash Forward

*Virginia Hamilton, interview on promotional video, Open Road Media, *Meet Virginia Hamilton,* uploaded April 20, 2011, www.youtube.com/watch?v =AyP5ZOMEn6c.

1. Mikkelsen, *Virginia Hamilton,* 88.

2. Ibid., 20.

3. Virginia Hamilton, "Thoughts on Children's Books, Reading, and Ethnic America." In *Perspectives in Reading No. 16: Reading, Children's Books, and Our Pluralistic Society,* ed. Harold Tanyzer and Jean Karl, prepared for a Joint Committee of the International Reading Association and Children's Book Council, 1972. From *Speeches, Essays, and Conversations,* 26.

4. National Book Foundation website, www.nationalbook.org.

5. American Library Association website, www.ala.org/cskbookawards.

6. Virginia Hamilton, *Her Stories: African American Folktales, Fairy Tales, and True Tales* (New York: Blue Sky Press, 1995), xiii.

Chapter Eight: First Person

*Virginia Hamilton to Marilyn Apseloff, December 12, 1983, box 1, Virginia Hamilton Conference, Special Collections and Archives, Kent State University Libraries.

1. Proposal for the Virginia Hamilton Lectureship Series and accompanying correspondence from Marilyn Apseloff to Virginia Hamilton, December 6, 1983, box 1, Virginia Hamilton Conference, Kent State University Libraries.

2. Virginia Hamilton to Marilyn Apseloff, December 12, 1983, box 1, Virginia Hamilton Conference, Kent State University Libraries.

3. Virginia Hamilton. "The Spirit Spins: A Writer's Revolution" (lecture, first annual Virginia Hamilton Lectureship on Minority Group Experiences in Children's Literature, April 12, 1985). From *Speeches, Essays, and Conversations,* 115.

4. Ibid., 115.

5. Ibid., 124.

6. Email correspondence with Angela Johnson, January 22, 2016.

7. *Family and Friends: The Anniversary Virginia Hamilton Conference Commemorative Cookbook,* 2004.

Chapter Nine: Resolution

*Virginia Hamilton, "Address to the 1990 Graduating Class of Bank Street College of Education" (New York City, 1990). From *Speeches, Essays, and Conversations,* 186.

1. Virginia Hamilton, "Mission to Moscow," *School Library Journal* (February 1980). From *Speeches, Essays, and Conversations,* 71.

2. Ibid, 70.

3. Ibid, 74.

4. Ibid, 77.

5. Moscow Info. Website for visitors to Moscow.

6. Hamilton, "Mission to Moscow," 78.

7. Ibid., 79–81.

8. Ibid., 82.

9. Letter from Virginia Hamilton to Noriko Shima, April 27, 1978.

10. Letter from Virginia Hamilton to Noriko Shima, February 28, 1983.

11. Letter from Virginia Hamilton to Noriko Shima, September 4, 1980.

12. Email correspondence with Arnold Adoff, January 28, 2016.

13. Letter from Virginia Hamilton to Noriko Shima, January 2, 1984.

14. Letter from Virginia Hamilton to Noriko Shima, December 2, 1993.

15. Virginia Hamilton, Jaguar Journal.

16. Letter from Virginia Hamilton to Noriko Shima, June 20, 1983.

17. Hamilton, Virginia, "Hans Christian Andersen Award Acceptance Speech" (Berlin, 1992). From *Speeches, Essays, and Conversations,* 216.

18. Ibid., 218.

19. The National Museum of the US Air Force website, http://www.nationalmuseum.af.mil/.

Chapter Ten: Conclusion

*Miriam Hoffman and Eva Samuels, *Authors and Illustrators of Children's Books: Writings on Their Lives and Works* (New York: R. R. Bowker, 1972), 192.

1. Virginia Hamilton Papers, Manuscript Division, Library of Congress.

2. Leigh Hamilton, "Rememory." From *Speeches, Essays, and Conversations*, 344.

3. Phone interview with Arnold Adoff, January 12, 2016.

4. Ibid.

5. Email correspondence with Rudine Sims Bishop, January 20, 2016.

6. Rudine Sims Bishop, *Virginia Hamilton on Liberation Literature*, www.youtube.com/watch?v=I5xX8Vv1vtl.

7. Email correspondence with Rudine Sims Bishop, January 20, 2016.

8. The MacArthur Foundation website, https://www.macfound.org/programs/fellows/strategy.

9. Virginia Hamilton, "Travelers in Time: Past, Present, and to Come" (speech, CLNE, Cambridge University, Cambridge, England). In *Origins of Story: On Writing for Children*, ed. Barbara Harrison and Gregory Maguire (New York: Margaret K. McElderry Books, 1999). From *Speeches, Essays, and Conversations*, 178.

10. Email correspondence with Nikki Giovanni, January 25, 2016.

11. Email correspondence with Jerry Pinkney, February 16, 2016.

12. Email correspondence with Arnold Adoff, January 28, 2016.

13. Letter from Ashley Bryan, February 5, 2016.

14. Virginia Hamilton, *The Planet of Junior Brown* (New York: Macmillan, 1971), 200.

15. Hamilton, *Zeely*, 121.

Bibliography

Books

Two Hundred Years of Yellow Springs: A Collection of Articles First Published in the Yellow Springs News for the 2003 Bicentennial of Yellow Springs, Ohio. Yellow Springs, OH: Yellow Springs News, 2005.

Chadwick, Bruce. *Traveling the Underground Railroad.* Secaucus, NJ: Carol Publishing Group, 1999.

Dudley Gold, Susan. *Loving v. Virginia: Lifting the Ban Against Interracial Marriage.* Tarrytown, PA: Marshall Cavendish Benchmark, 2008.

Family and Friends: The Anniversary Virginia Hamilton Conference Commemorative Cookbook, 2004.

Fradin, David Brindell. *Bound for the North Star: True Stories of Fugitive Slaves.* New York: Clarion Books, 2000.

Galloway, William Albert. *The History of Glen Helen.* Yellow Springs, OH: Glen Helen Association, 1932.

Hamilton, Virginia. *Her Stories: African American Folk Tales, Fairy Tales, and Trued Tales.* New York: Blue Sky Press, 1995.

———. *The House of Dies Drear.* New York: Macmillan, 1968.

———. *M.C. Higgins, the Great.* New York: Macmillan, 1974.

———. *Paul Robeson: The Life and Times of a Free Black Man.* New York: Harper & Row, 1974.

———. *The Planet of Junior Brown.* New York: Macmillan, 1971.

———. *Speeches, Essays, and Conversations.* Edited by Arnold Adoff and Kacy Cook. New York: Blue Sky Press, 2010.

———. *The Time-Ago Tales of Jahdu.* New York: Macmillan, 1969.

———. *W. E. B. DuBois: A Biography.* New York: Thomas Y. Crowell, 1972.

———. *Zeely.* New York: Macmillan, 1967.

Hoffman, Miriam, and Eva Samuels. *Authors and Illustrators of Children's Books: Writings on Their Lives and Works.* New York: R. R. Bowker, 1972.

Jewell, Elizabeth J., and Frank Abate, eds. *The New Oxford American Dictionary.* New York: Oxford University Press, 2001.

Mayer, Robert H. *When the Children Marched: The Birmingham Civil Rights Movement.* Berkeley Heights, NJ: Enslow, 2008.

Middleton, Stephen. *The Black Laws: Race and the Legal Process in Early Ohio.* Athens: Ohio University Press, 2005.

Mikkelsen, Nina. *Virginia Hamilton.* New York: Twayne, 1994.

Quillin, Frank. *The Color Line in Ohio: A History of Race Prejudice in a Typical Northern State.* Ann Arbor: University of Michigan Press, 1913.

Essays

Adoff, Arnold. "Arnold: Late at Night in Ginny's Office." In *Speeches, Essays, and Conversations,* edited by Arnold Adoff and Kacy Cook. New York: Blue Sky Press, 2010.

Adoff, Leigh. "Rememory." In *Speeches, Essays, and Conversations.*

Hamilton, Virginia. "AH, Sweet Rememory." In *Horn Book Magazine.* Reprinted in *Speeches, Essays, and Conversations.*

———. "Changing Woman, Working." In *Celebrating Children's Books: Essays on Children's Literature in Honor of Zena Sutherland,* edited by Betsy Hearne and Marilyn Kaye. New York: Lothrop, Lee & Shepard Books, 1981. Reprinted in *Speeches, Essays, and Conversations.*

———. "Mission to Moscow." In *School Library Journal,* February 1980. Reprinted in *Speeches, Essays, and Conversations.*

———. "Portrait of the Author as a Working Writer." In *Elementary English,* an official publication of the National Council of Teachers of English, April 1971. Reprinted in *Speeches, Essays, and Conversations.*

Speeches

Hamilton, Virginia. "Address to the 1990 Graduating Class of Bank Street College of Education." Presented in New York City, 1990. In *Speeches, Essays, and Conversations.*

———. "Coretta Scott King Award Acceptance Speech: *Sweet Whispers, Brother Rush.*" Presented at the American Library Conference, 1983. In *Speeches, Essays, and Conversations.*

———. "Further Notes on a Progeny's Progress." Speech delivered at the Children and Young People's Meeting of the New Jersey Library Association, May 4, 1968. In *Speeches, Essays, and Conversations.*

———. "Hans Christian Andersen Award Acceptance Speech." Presented in Berlin, 1992. In *Speeches, Essays, and Conversations.*

———. "Illusions and Reality." Lecture presented at Library of Congress, Washington DC, November 17, 1975. In *Speeches, Essays, and Conversations.*

———. "Literature, Creativity, and Imagination." Speech delivered at George Peabody College for Teachers, Nashville, TN, 1972. In *Speeches, Essays, and Conversations.*

———. "Newbery Award Acceptance Speech: *M.C. Higgins, the Great.*" Presented at the American Library Association meeting, San Francisco, CA, 1975. In *Speeches, Essays, and Conversations.*

———. "Coretta Scott King Award Acceptance Speech: *The People Could Fly: American Black Folktales.*" Presented at the American Library Association conference, New York City, 1986. In *Speeches, Essays, and Conversations.*

———. "Reflections." The Marygrove College Contemporary American Authors Lecture, Detroit, MI, April 1997. In *Speeches, Essays, and Conversations.*

———. "Regina Medal Acceptance Speech." Presented to the Catholic Library Association, 1990. In *Speeches, Essays, and Conversations.*

———. "The Spirit Spins: A Writer's Revolution." Lecture for the first annual Virginia Hamilton Lectureship on Minority Group Experiences in Children's Literature, April 12, 1985. In *Speeches, Essays, and Conversations.*

———. "Travelers in Time: Past, Present, and to Come." CLNE, Cambridge University, Cambridge, England. In *Origins of Story: On Writing for Children*, edited by Barbara Harrison and Gregory Maguire. New York: Margaret K. McElderry Books, 1999. Reprinted in *Speeches, Essays, and Conversations.*

Articles

Andeen, Ashley, and John Lesley King. "Addressing and the Future of Communications Competition: Lessons from the Telephony and the Internet." *Information Infrastructure and Policy* 6, no. 1, IOS Press (1998).

Bishop, Rudine Sims. "Books from Parallel Cultures: Celebrating a Silver Anniversary." *Horn Book Magazine* 69, no. 2 (March/April 1993).

———. "Virginia Hamilton." *Horn Book Magazine* 71, no. 4 (July/August, 1995).

Chiddister, Diane. "A History of Racial Diversity." *Yellow Springs News*, February 10, 2010.

———. "Tecumseh and the Yellow Spring." *Yellow Springs News*. Reprinted in *Two Hundred Years of Yellow Springs*. Yellow Springs: Yellow Springs News, 2005.

Dayton Daily News. "People Alone." October 16, 1977.

Hamilton, Virginia. "Planting Seeds." *Horn Book Magazine* 68, no. 6 (November 1992).

———. "Sentinels in Long Still Rows." *American Libraries* 30, no. 6 (June/July 1999).

———. "Thoughts on Children's Books, Reading, and Ethnic America." In *Perspectives in Reading No. 16: Reading, Children's Books, and our Pluralistic Society*, compiled and edited by Harold Tanyzer and Jean Karl, prepared for a Joint Committee of the International Reading Association and Children's Book Council, 1972. Reprinted in *Speeches, Essays, and Conversations*.

McInnis, Doug. "Focus: Muskingum County, Ohio: From Strip Mine to African Game Preserve." *New York Times,* June 25, 1989.

Petsonk, Judy. "Writer harnesses powerful prose with discipline." *Dayton Daily News,* May 16, 1976.

Wallis, Don. "Where's *The House of Dies Drear*? Virginia Hamilton's Imagination." *Yellow Spring News*, November 21, 1984.

Thesis

Quillin, Frank. 1913. "The Color Line in Ohio: A History of Race Prejudice in a Typical Northern State." Thesis, University of Michigan, Ann Arbor.

Interviews

Adoff, Arnold. June 4 and September 15–16, 2015.

Adoff, Arnold. Various phone interviews.

Hamilton, Virginia. *Meet Virginia Hamilton*. Interview on promotional video, Open Road Media, www.youtube.com/watch?v=AyP5ZOMEn6c, uploaded April 20, 2011.

Virginia Hamilton on Liberation Literature. Interview on promotional video, www.youtube.com/watch?v=I5xX8Vv1vtl.

Manuscript Collections

Virginia Hamilton Conference. Special Collections and Archives, Kent State University Libraries, Kent, Ohio.
Virginia Hamilton Papers. Manuscript Division, Library of Congress.

Correspondence

Adoff, Arnold. Email to author, November 5, 2015.
Bishop, Rudine Sims. Email to author, January 19, 2016.
Bryan, Ashley. Letter to author, February 5, 2016.
Giovanni, Nikki. Email to author, January 25, 2016.
Hamilton, Virginia. Letter to Ellen Rudin, November 15, 1974.
Hamilton, Virginia. Letters to Noriko Shima.
Johnson, Angela. Email to author, January 22, 2016.

Websites

American Library Association. www.ala.org/cskbookawards.
Virginia Hamilton. www.virginiahamilton.com.
International Board on Books for Children. www.ibby.org.
MacArthur Foundation. www.macfound.org/programs/fellows/strategy.
Moscow.Info.
National Book Foundation. www.nationalbook.org.
National Museum of the US Air Force. www.nationalmuseum.af.mil/.
Scholastic Publishers. www.scholastic.com
The Wilds. www.thewilds.columbuszoo.org.

Additional Resources

In addition to the resources above, the author was granted access to the following archives:
Greene County Public Library.
Arnold Adoff provided the author with photographs, correspondence, and wonderful memories and stories.

BIOGRAPHIES FOR YOUNG READERS

Michelle Houts, Series Editor